SAN FRANCISCO POEMS

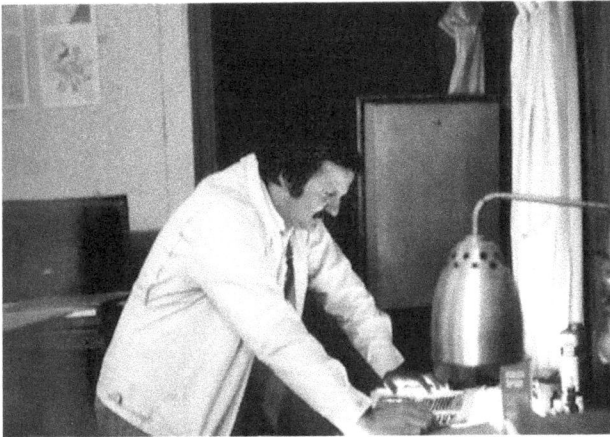

A.D. Winans. Photo by Wilfredo Castano.

SAN FRANCISCO POEMS

BY

A.D. WINANS

SECOND EDITION

Little Red Tree Publishing, LLC,
509 W 3rd Street, North Platte, NE.

Published Books by A.D. Winans: 1970-2016

Carmel Clowns (1970)
Crazy John Poems (1972)
Straws Of Sanity (1975)
Tales of Crazy John (1976)
North Beach Poems (1977)
ORG-1 (1977)
All the Graffiti On All The Bathroom Walls
        Can't Hide These Scars Of Mine (1977)
The Further Adventures of Crazy John (1980)
The Reagan Psalms (1984)
In Memoriam (1990)
A Knife In the Heart And Jazz In My Soul (1996)
The Land Is Not My Land (1996)
The Charles Bukowski Second Coming Years (1996)
Love Comes In Many Different Flavors (1997)
It Serves You Right To Suffer (1997)
A Call To Poets (1997)
San Francisco Streets (1997)
Venus In Pisces (1997)
Remembering Jack Micheline (1998)
America (1998)
Looking For An Answer (1998)
From Pussy To Politics (1999)
Remembering Bukowski (1999)
People You think You know (1999)
North Beach Revisited (2000)
13 Jazz Poems (2001)
City Blues (2001)
I Kiss The Feet Of Angels (2001)
The Holy Grail: Charles Bukowski And The Second
        Coming Revolution. (2002)
Whispers From Hell (2002)
Will the Real Lawrence Ferlinghetti Please Stand Up (2002)
Trying To Find A Common Bond (2002)
A Bastard Child With No Place To Go (2002)

The System (2003)
A.D. Winans' Greatest Hits: 1995-2003 (2003)
Whitman's Lost Children ((2004)
The Wrong Side Of Town (bilingual. English/Russian) (2004)
Dreams That Won't Leave Me Alone (2004)
In Memoriam: New and Selected Poems (2004)
The Wrong Side Of Town (2005)
This Land Is Not My Land (2005)
The World's Last Rodeo (2006)
South of Market Street (2006)
Tombstone Graffiti 2006)
The Other Side Of Broadway: Selected Poems: 1965-1995. (2007)
Marking Time (2008)
Days In Heaven Nights In Hell (2009)
Billie Holiday Me And The Blues (2009)
No Room For Buddha (2009)
Pigeon Feathers (2009)
Love – Zero (2010)
Dancing With Words (2010)
Black Lily (2010)
Drowning Like Li Po In a River of Red Wine:
        Selected Poems: 1970-2010 (2010)
The Show Must Go On (2010)
San Francisco Poems (2011) 1st Edition
Wind On His Wings (2012)
In the Dead Hours of Dawn (2013)
Dead Lions (Memoir) (2014)
In the Pink (Short Story collection) (2014)
This Land Is Not My Land (2015) 2nd Edition
San Francisco Poems (2017) 2nd Edition

Second Edition, 2017, manufactured in USA
1 2 3 4 5 6 7 8 9 10 LSI   23 22 21 20 19 18 17

Fonts used: Minion Pro, Times Roman, Trajan Pro and Ariel.

Cover and Book Design:
Michael John Linnard, MCSD

Front Cover photograph "Golden Gate Bridge" [2008] by Martin Künzel and reproduced here under GNU Free Documentation License.

Some of the poems in this book were originally published by *The New York Quarterly, Primal Urge, BOS Press, Erbacee Press, Editions Microbe, 24th Street Irregular Press and Second Coming.*

The prologue was originally published in the *Contemporary Authors Autobiography Series*, Volume 28, by Gale Research, in a slightly different version.

Library of Congress Cataloging-in-Publication Data

Names: Winans, A. D., author.
Title: San Francisco poems / by A. D. Winans.
Description: Second edition. | North Platte, NE : Little Red Tree
  Publishing, 2017. | Includes index.
Identifiers: LCCN 2017026552 | ISBN 9781935656487 (pbk. : alk. paper)
Subjects: LCSH: San Francisco (Calif.)--Poetry
Classification: LCC PS3573.I4787 A6 2017 | DDC 811/.54--dc23
LC record available at https://lccn.loc.gov/2017026552

Little Red Tree Publishing, LLC
509 W 3rd Street, North Platte, NE
website: www.littleredtree.com

CONTENTS

Introduction by Charles Plymel   xi

Prologue by A.D. Winans   1

I am San Francisco	39
City Poet	43
Going Back In Time	44
The Wrong Side of Town	45
Saturday Night Special	46
Saturday Night Happenings	47
Remembering	48
Cocaine Annie	49
South of Market	50
Chinatown Sweat Shop	51
d.a.Levy Was Dead Right	52
For Jamie	53
The Black Hawk 1963	54
Jazz Angel	55
Memories	56
Old Warrior of North Beach	57
Old Joe	58
For Jack Micheline	59
Poem for Alexsey Dayen	60
San Francisco Streets	61
Thank God for Small Favors	63
City Happenings	64
Post Office Reflection	65
South of Market Blues	66
Aquatic Park Poem	67
Looking Back	68
A Matter of Trust	70
Girls of the Tenderloin	71
Burning Old Poems	72
Woman on the Balcony	73
New Years Eve Poem 2010	74
Jim's Donut Shop	75
Sitting At the 3300 Club	76

Mission Street Bar	77
Eastern Zen and Pig Pen	78
Eating Chinese	79
40th Birthday Poem	80
Poem for the Poet Waiting on Fame	82
Walking the Mission on a Hot Sunday Afternoon	84
Walking the Streets Like a Cowboy Looking for a Miracle	85
Open Your Eyes	86
Under the Light of a Full Moon	88
Survival Song	92
Media Blues	94
Six AM Poem	95
Poem for the Poets Who Feast on the Flesh of the Dead	96
Old Men of Skid Row	97
Wasted Days Wasted Nights	98
Christmas 1996	99
Tenderloin Cafeteria Poem II	100
Fourth of July Poem	101
Poem for the Governor of Arizona	104
Fillmore Blues	105
Outside a Boarded Down Jazz Club	106
Ocean Beach	107
Poem for an Imaginary Daughter	108
Un Titled	109
State of Affairs	110
Lost Summer of Love	111
Sometimes the Words Just Won't Come	112
Thoughts on the California Drought	113
It's How You Look At It	114
For Kell	115
Tenderloin Cafeteria Poem	117
Poem for the Poet the Working Man and the Upper Mobile Yuppie	118
Thinking About Then and Now	119
Returning Home From Panama	120
I Have Loitered	121
Vietnam Winter Reflections	122
Poem for Paddy O'Sullivan	123
Poem for a Friend Who Told Me I Need to Stop	

Dwelling on the Past   125
It Serves You Right To Suffer   128
Life on the Streets   130
North Beach Yuppie Bar   132
Remembering My Grandmother   133
Dining Out When I Was Young   135
Early Morning San Francisco   136
Martha's Coffee Shop   138
The Old Italians of Aquatic Park   139
San Francisco Blues   141
No Questions Asked   143
For Jill   145
Let's Get Real   146
One Too Many Poets   149
Poem for my First Love   151
From My Window   152
Insomnia   154
66   155
Seventy   156
Seventy-One   157
Winter Poem   158
Dining Out When I Was Young   159
Random Word Poem   160
Back from an MRI   161
Monday Morning Poem   162
The Worlds Last Rodeo   163
Poem for a Friend In Prison   164
How I Want to be Remembered   167
Hospital Poem   168
New Years Day Poem   170
Poem for Jack Micheline   171
Ghosts from the Past   174
Waste Land of Blurred Visions   176
Call to Poets   179
Winter Poem II   182
Trump Land   184

Index of Poems   185
About the Author   192

INTRODUCTION

Feminine force has sometimes been assigned to that beautiful City by the Bay, so it's natural it undergoes periodical changes. It is sometimes forgotten that it's a port, and, one it seems for every stormy life that landed there. A.D. Winans is the first person I know who was born in San Francisco. During my love affair(s) there, it seemed I lived on all her streets, climbed her hills and while high on top of Twin Peaks, marveled at her jewel-like lights strung on streets below. She is almost surrounded by water; a fact the poet Lew Welch often reminded me of. Fog could intertwine in the breath of sailors sipping martinis at the Top of the Mark, as I watched ships pass each other as lovers in the night, a reminder of the old Barbary Coast, or Mammy Pleasant building her neighborhoods through sex slaves and transients, newer captives with each experience a lifetime etched in memory. I certainly left my heart there, at least the presentiment that makes the heart see quicker than the eye. It demands an extraordinary vision to record this city. A.D. Winans has brought its inhabitants to life again for another look, however quick, however deep.

My sister, who died on the street there in front of an Indian bar was a transient, I was a transient, certainly the people of the tribes were transient as a Chinese lantern of the western moon, but the city always gave up its special feeling of home with all that implies. I met the Frisco Kid back east at a book convention some years later. It took until this day to realize he was a native to this city, and in his poems he identifies places he went as a child that I was to know later and stake a claim to the magical image that always changed yet remained steady.

As presentiment is to heart, sensitivity is to creativity and the transient nature of this most beautiful city became the fiction that shed periodically like the snakeskin, the lines of itself. Crooners claim to have indeed left their hearts there. Soul singers and philosophers worked on the docks. Jazz claimed it; Opera claimed it; Movies claimed it; Detective Novels claimed it; Rock and Roll claimed it (even built on it) Religious Vision claimed it; Madness claimed it; and yes Poetry claimed it! Even the Police claimed it.

A.D. Winans lived it. "His mind destroyed by shock treatments/ And one too many police batons." It was always the large canvas artist forever recorded lines where the real and unreal blurred and sometimes struck. Winans warns, "Never place your hand over/ your heart the/Marksman might think/ you're marking his target..."

There were /are many different kinds of poets who gravitated into that feminine energy. Like fish they traveled in two, even in schools, or more notably cliques. San Francisco was a natural basin for poets and was even known for destroying itself at times. When I arrived there, older poets I admired like Rexroth and Patchen were closing shop. On arriving in the city, Dave Haselwood, a fellow Kansan, gave me a copy of John Weiner's Hotel Wently Poems (which A.D. Winans says was an influence on his own writing). It was during a short stay there that I had an altercation with a sailor and Neal Cassady in Anne's room and would eat a rather naked lunch with Leary and Ginsberg below the hotel at Foster's Cafeteria in "Polk Gulch." Events in that city seemed linked, too, a fishnet never quite ending.

Rexroth organized the famous reading of Howl in the '5Os that led to the famous obscenity trial where Ginsberg's vision of Marlon Brando, the Icon of the year, led to such hyperbole, even the best minds of San Francisco became forever obsessed. To this day, City Lights Bookstore enjoys the tourist trade from the publicity of the trial. While the author certainly didn't "abandon" his moloch and had no reserve for taking thousands from "Moloch the stunned governments," it changed lives with such force as to create a Beatnik millionaire from a Navy officer and graduate of the Sorbonne, Lawrence Ferlinghetti. A similar institution arose in the Fillmore by another NYC city cat Bill Graham who saw fame in the old Palladium and plunged his vision to the depths of this city. To imagine being a poet who was born in and grew up in this city is to see a history that A.D. Winans records so accurately through his poetry.

While poets protested against money and government while building religious and sexual constituencies in visionary fervor, or became jaded, or "trippy" Winans kept his style. Jack Spicer frequented and conversed with Winans at Gino & Carlos. Jack Micheline, his friend, who had the chops, wanted to really turn over those ash cans of millionaire dollars seen prudishly by

Ginsberg as "Filth! Ugliness!" before the politically correct safe, academic mainstream took over. Turf also didn't bother another of A.D. Winans's friends, the late George Tsongas. Tsongas wasn't a political poet, but he talked politics every day. I, like them, didn't care for the labels. I could see as much in a Wyeth as in a Blake. The scene shifted again towards the Haight Ashbury (where A.D. Winans grew up a child). The Go-Go clubs flourished while Sonny Rollins played at North Beach dives for a two-drink minimum. At the old Avalon Ballroom I saw a handful of hippies turn out to hear an "unknown" Bo Diddley. Meanwhile, if one looked closer at Winans's poetry, there were constants. "I have observed old women/fumble in broken down purses/for non existent dreams." In the city where Winans was born, he grew up with those truths that were etched in faces that changed as well, but probably not what the tourists were seeing.

I don't know if poets see differently than other folks. I have certainly been in the presence of some who missed what I saw, and I've certainly seen things I didn't want to see. It's obvious some poets are compelled to write what they didn't want to see in the first place. That was the impression I had from Bob Kaufman, one of Winans's companions, who took a vow of silence. In *San Francisco Poems* Winans records a lifetime of the streets. They are photographic in that they can see a line in a face added by time, even the atavistic lines, that might cause one to avert one's eyes. For his is the city of many poets, and as Robert Peters offered, "poetry munchkins." So there is definitely turf. But Winans reminds us "...that every meat packer/And fisherman, every waitress/And construction worker, knows more/About life than your average poet." I connect with Winans's poetry in memories when I walked the streets south of Market down to the docks always in pairs, if not in groups, with our longshoreman hooks prominently displayed in our belts, for it's an area a tourist would go at his peril, and poets, not that many. But Winans is one of them who did.

> "You can see from the
> Look in his eyes the
> Scar on his face
> That he's someone

You don't want to mess with
His eyes survey the scene
Like a periscope

He's a two-bit thug
Looking for action
An old beat cop looking
For a head to bash
He's Boston Blackie
And Al Capone rolled into one..."

In these lines, Winans not only reveals the faces on the street, but the tragedy therein, where a transient, like Jack Black could find a home. Where the hoboes, hookers, "rounders," and finally hipster poets came to the tenderloin, walked on Turk Street, and ate at Compton's Cafeteria. Her history keeps sucking up the changes, the tragedies of every phony, every dreamer, every hero, and every loser. And Winans's city is unique with the many poets it has embraced. Harte Crane didn't have that situation in Akron. And within that change, that turf, that carnival, that mainstream of visionary-cum-academic, there is an importance to me that I claimed as my home, that space no matter the physical changes, there was the emotion of that space, the space Winans keeps occupied with his poems, that street where my epiphany is his and the poets he knew. It's the hometown he saw both as a child and as a grown up, that very scene that must be read by its inhabitants, its tourists who run into the bookstore, or its poets who must live the boundless postcard, however briefly.

"I have sat
One too many evenings watching
Old men and women
Eat their last meal
One eye on the desert the
Other on the obituary column"

Charles Plymell,
Cherry Valley, NY, 2010

A.D. Winans, a photograph by Alexsey Dayen.

PROLOGUE

I find it difficult talking about myself. No matter how hard I try, it sounds self-serving. I prefer to let my poems do the talking. Too many poets perceive their craft as a holy mission, seeing themselves as prophets. That's a hard message to sell to the homeless and downtrodden souls that walk the streets of our inner cities, or the working-class men and women struggling to make ends meet. My poetry largely addresses issues of concern to millions of Americans who spend their lives struggling to survive in a society, bankrupt in spirit and moral fiber, where money is the only common denominator.

My literary mentors are Jack Micheline, the late Charles Bukowski, and the late Bob Kaufman, although early on I was influenced by William Carlos Williams and the Beat poet John Weiners, whose *Hotel Wentley* poems moved me deeply. I am indebted to William Carlos Williams who advised poets to "Write like you speak."

I have never worn the label of poet well. It's not a word I'm comfortable with. I sometimes think I'm possessed by demons whose voices confront me whenever I sit down to write. The finished poem often bears little resemblance to whatever I initially had in mind. The demon voices simply invade my thought process and take over. I share Jack Spicer's philosophy that verse does not originate from within the poet's expressive will as a spontaneous gesture mediated by formal constraints, but is "a foreign agent, a parasite that invades the poet's language and expresses what it wants to say."

I've never kept a notebook or used a tape recorder for later reference. I seldom write in longhand. This isn't my style.

I have been both blessed and cursed by the inner voices (demons) that possess me. I'm a prolific poet and writer, capable of producing large amounts of work in a short period of time, and then slacking off for long periods of time.

I have been called a "street poet" by many people. I suppose this is because many of my poems deal with life on the streets. I don't think this is an accurate label. I have been writing for over four decades, and my style continues to evolve. The subject matter ranges from political and social commentary to humor, haiku, and surrealism, but the form and technique I employ is not always the same.

I like to think of myself in baseball terms. Just when the batter thinks he has me figured out, I change from a fastball to a hard slider, or a wicked curve, occasionally throwing in a change-up to confuse him.

I think a good poet has to experiment with different forms or be left behind. At seventy-five, I'm still growing, and no closer to seeing the light at the end of the tunnel than I was when I penned my first poem. The one constant is that people remain my favorite subject matter. If Weiners is, in fact, a poet's poet, I'd like to be remembered as the people's poet.

My poems and my life are one and the same. They simply can't be separated. Let me quote from a few poets and writers who have gained some insight into me.

Neeli Cherkovski wrote, "You're one hell of a wordslinger . . . a truly exceptional open word open form right from the art of the heart poet . . . strong in the wreck of the years as they come down upon us." Neeli sees me as a warrior who has paid his dues. I don't know if I have paid my dues or not, but I'm working on it.

I was born in San Francisco and know the streets of the city and its diverse faces the way a gambler knows when to hold and when to fold. Jack Micheline said, "A.D. Winans is a man in search of his soul. His compassion and love for his native city San Francisco shows in his poems. A.D. takes us on a journey of lost souls in the cruelty of a large city. He writes of the people he loves: poets,

Jack Micheline and A.D. SF. Photo by Linda Lerner

musicians, and the ordinary souls who have moved him.

"A.D. Winans loves San Francisco. He knows the wars, the lost hookers, the crazies, the victims, and the ones gone mad. The system and the tragedy of America."

That's high praise from a poet I deeply respect. Here's a poem I wrote in 1996 on my native city. See for yourself if Micheline is right or not.

San Francisco Streets

I have walked these streets
Like a cop walks his beat
My eyes taking in her every movement
My brain storing real and imagined changes
In sixty years her changes have not eluded me
She is older now
More wrinkled and cranky much like me
But the two of us manage to get along
Like business partners looking after the others interest

Market Street once a fashionable socialite
Now a gaudy whore
Mission Street once the home of the Irish
Now glossed over
Tough looking youths with dagger stares
Where you guard your wallet
Like a eunuch guards the harem door

You have to learn to give and take
You have to learn to adjust
The city is like a cup of strong coffee
Stir her enough and the flavor floats
To the top

I have walked these streets all my life
In good condition and broken down physique
Knowing there is no city like her in the world
She is like a pair of empty shoes
Sitting under the bed

With no feet big enough to fill them
She is like a squirrel running between
The live wires of a utility poll
She is like the last bullet in the
Executioner's gun
She is like a room full of poets
Crazed with their own conversation
She is like Billie Holiday drenched in sweat
She is like the face of God
All forgiving in her insatiable lust
For life

"Antler," a fellow poet, has said: "I love your poems that deal with the legendary city of, romantics, adventure, and homelessness desperation.

"As a long time life-long poet you, to me, represent a survivor who persevered in spite of the bummers of the poetry scene and disillusionment with poet heroes and mentors.

"Your poems and personality seem free of the bitterness and enmity I've seen possess so many poets after the age of fifty. Beneath everything, above everything, in your work seems a human compassion toward the human drama and its humane compassion toward its actors and actresses."

My sister Barbara and me. Photo by Allan Winans, Senior.

It sounds less self-serving, hearing someone else say these words. This is why I chose to present the words of others who have captured my spirit and what it is that I'm trying to do in my writing.

I'm not a guru. I don't go to the mountains looking for the Dalai Lama. I create largely in isolation. I don't long for academic recognition. Neither do I see the academic world as my enemy, as Bukowski did.

I write out of a sense of loneliness and sadness and anger, but also with humor. In this I am indebted to Bob Kaufman. I write with the same observational power and with the same intensity as Charles Bukowski, yet entirely unlike Bukowski. You don't need a dictionary to understand my poems. I write from the heart. I try in the most direct manner possible to say the things I have seen and experienced in life, and hope that the reader will find the voyage a memorable one.

I'm sure many poets, including many academics, see my poems in a simplistic light, to be dismissed. Bukowski was faced with a similar ignorance. To these people, I would simply quote from Colin Wilson: "Everything I read by A.D. Winans fills me with pleasure because of a beautiful natural and easy use of language— he seems to have an ability which should be common but which is in fact very rare to somehow allow his own pleasant personality to flow direct into the page."

It's true that I write poetry using a natural and easy use of language because this is the way I believe poetry should be written. I'm afraid, however, that my personality isn't always pleasant. Sometimes the anger cuts through and severs an artery, but I believe this only serves to make the poem stronger. How can one not be angry at what is happening in this great land of ours: the homeless, random drive-by gang shootings, the drug epidemic, and aids, and an unjust economic structure.

We are experiencing a time when the top 1% of the wealthiest individuals in the country are prospering while the middle class wages have remained stagnant or dropped in purchasing power.

Corporations continue to make obscene profits while downsizing the workforce. Right wing governors encouraged by the tea party are passing laws limiting or eliminating collective bargaining for the work force. Civil rights won in the 1960s are being threatened by immoral politicians who wave flags in our faces while accepting illegal campaign funds. Unemployment figures are being manipulated to make the economy seem better than it really is. Poor whites and blacks are being brainwashed into believing that immigrants are responsible for their troubles. Given these circumstances, how could I not be angry?

When William Faulkner gave his Nobel Literature Prize acceptance speech, he said:

"I believe that man will not merely endure, he will prevail. He is immortal, not because he alone among creature, has an inexhaustible voice, but because he has a soul, a spirt, capable of compassion and sacrifice and endurance. The poet's, the writer's duty, is to write about these things. It is his privilege to help man endure by lifting his heart, by reminding him of courage and honor and hope and pride and compassion and pity. The poet's voice need not merely be the record of man; it can be one of the props to help him endure and prevail."

I write about life, its ups and downs. The laughter and the tears. The real and the imagined. The good in man and the evil in man. I don't pull any punches. I simply try to tell it like it is, from the bombing of the Federal Building in Oklahoma to the American experiences in Vietnam and Iraq.

That old adage that anyone in America can be anything they want to be is a lie. I speak about this in a poem.

The System

There are old men and women
Who have worked all their lives
Who have put in three four decades
For the right to a pension
There are old people who have
Worked twenty years or more
Only to be laid off and given
Two weeks severance pay
To seek a living at half the pay
There are old people who have
Worked all their lives only
To witness the company go belly-up
And find there is no pension fund left
You can find them on park benches
Or wandering sterile supermarkets
Or sitting at neighborhood bars

Nursing their drinks like
A blood transfusion
They come in assorted flavors
Like Life Savers
Some thin and balding
Some fat and sweating
Some complaining bitterly
Some too proud to let the pain show
So proud they eat dog food
Finding dessert in back alley
Garbage cans
Trapped by a belief in a system
That has abandoned them

For the most part they suffer
In silence, duly unnoticed
To be carted off in meat wagons
To be cut open by coroners
Who see them as morning cereal
Who go about their business
Like a butcher
Thinking of dinner
Thinking of a glass of wine
Thinking of how it used to be
How it might have been
How it should have been

It's the way of life
It's the way of politicians
And mice
It ain't pretty
It ain't nice
It's the system where
Just trying to stay alive
Becomes a small victory

I didn't start out writing poetry. Like Bukowski, I wrote short
stories and submitted them to slick magazines like *Harper's* and

Mother, Claire

the *Atlantic.* They came back with the standard rejection slips, which I pasted on the walls of my small apartment located in the Western Addition of San Francisco. I turned to *Evergreen Review* and *Avant Garde* magazine, with similar results, except for the occasional handwritten rejection slip, encouraging further submissions.

I sold my first short story for five dollars to the *Mendocino Robin.* A short time later I sold my first poem to *Poetry Australia* for ten dollars. A week later *Avant Garde* mailed me back a story I had submitted with the following comment: "Your style reminds us a lot of Vonnegut and he's no slouch, but it isn't what the boss is looking for."

I decided to concentrate on poetry, which has always come easier to me, unlike fiction, which I find a need to constantly revise.

I made North Beach my home away from home from 1958 through much of the eighties but never considered myself a Beat poet or writer. If one must use labels, I would prefer the label of bohemian.

T. S. Eliot and William Carlos Williams were two of the earliest poets to influence me. However, it was jazz and jazz musicians like Thelonius Monk, John Coltrane, Leadbelly, and Miles Davis that excited me early on. The *Evergreen Review* was one of the first literary magazines I read with regularity. It was around this same time that I discovered the work of William Everson (Brother Antoninus) and John Weiners.

We are all products of our upbringing. I was born at home, in San Francisco, a premature child. My father was seventeen years older than my mother, and they fought all the time. Whenever my mother wasn't yelling at my father, she was yelling at me.

My mother was born in Canada and was smuggled illegally into the United States when she was only three years old. When she tried to become a U.S. citizen, she was told by immigration officials that there was no records of her entry into the United States and was advised by custom officials not to pursue the matter or she might face deportation. She died a woman without a country.

Memories

It wasn't until after my mother died
That I learned as a child
She had been abused which helps
To explain why she slept all those years
With her clothes on
The memories linger inside me
The fighting that had no end
My parents like Joe Louis and Max Baer
Going the full fifteen rounds until
I grew up avoiding relationships
It wasn't until I turned fifty that
I realized I was holding a loaded gun
To the head of every woman
I might have loved
Squeezing off live rounds of an
Angry childhood
The seeds I left behind in
Those vaginas were bullets
Meant for my mother's womb

Father, Allan Winans, Sr

My father had a difficult time expressing himself. I don't recall him ever saying he loved me or my sister. It was my mother who took me for walks in the park and to the movies. My father didn't like his job as a conductor on the Muni Railway and frequently called in sick.

As a young boy, I remember hearing on the radio that the Japanese had bombed Pearl Harbor. I was too young to understand the full implications of war, but knew it had to be evil. Businesses had signs posted like, "Loose Lips Sink Ships," and homes had flags in the window. If a family had a son fighting in the war, a tiny star appeared on the flag, and if the star was gold, it was a sign that a son had died. There were minor inconveniences, like shortages of butter, sugar, and meat. The government issued ration books and tiny red tokens, which were used when you went to the grocery store or butcher shop to buy the staples of life.

Our family would gather in the living room and listen to our favorite radio shows: The *Green Hornet* and The *Lone Ranger*, to name a few. We saved lard in coffee cans and took the filled cans to the corner butcher shop. My father said the lard was used to grease the guns for the young men who were fighting over-seas, but this turned out to be a myth.

My parents brought me and my sister up to be tolerant of racial and religious differences, but all around me kids were using word like *nips* and *krauts*.

I enjoyed the Saturday movie matinees, especially the weekly serials at the Haight Theater that kept me glued to the edge of my seat.

The day the war ended, my parents sent me and my sister to bed early. I learned later that thousands of people had gone crazy in the streets of downtown San Francisco. What started out as joyful celebration turned into a riot, after a teenage girl was raped in a department store display window, in front of a cheering crowd. The police had to call in the National Guard, and the city was placed under martial law. Peace wasn't restored for several weeks.

My grandparents and I weren't close. My grandfather spent most of his time sitting in his rocking chair listening to classical records that he played on an old windup Victrola. My grandmother didn't get along with my mother. She was a diabetic (anemic) and had to eat raw liver for her condition. It was my grandmother who bought me my first typewriter and encouraged me to become a writer.

Poem for My Grandmother

A swirling mist blows through my ears
Filling me with strange notions
Bringing me back to my childhood
How the devil demons invaded my head
Chasing mad dinosaurs through dark alleys
Pausing to drink from my thirsty lips
All knowledge passed on down to me
By well-meaning parents
Who insisted that dinosaurs didn't exist
Grandmother was eaten alive by one
She knew what I meant

The last apartment house we lived in before my parents bought a home was on Page Street, near Golden Gate Park. Ceil, the landlord's wife, became my mother's only real friend. Ceil's daughter Dolores and I became inseparable. We did practically everything together. She was the first girl to show me the difference between boys and girls.

My sister was a tomboy and the apple of my father's eye. She was a straight-A student and belonged to the high school drama club and won the Chamber of Commerce Junior Achievement Award in her junior year. I chose a different route becoming the class clown and the biggest pop off in school.

As a child, I liked the Sunday drives we took to Alum Park. We would spend the early morning hours in the kitchen preparing a picnic lunch. I always made sure there was a heap of ice in the portable ice chest, during the long drive, I would suck on ice cubes until my gums were numb. It drove my mother crazy. It was so cramped in the car that I looked at these outings with mixed emotions, but it presented a welcome opportunity to break up the daily routine.

My first year at Dudley Stone Grammar School was hell. I walked up the stairs of the school and saw it as a fortress. The walls seemed to me a means of making sure you couldn't escape. The courtyard had a wire fence around it. It made me feel like I was in a concentration camp.

I didn't do well at Dudley Stone. My first-grade teacher didn't like me. I don't recall, but they said I dipped the pigtails of girls in the desk inkwells and was in the process of being punished when my parents removed my sister and me from Dudley Stone and enrolled us in a private school, the Pillar of Fire.

I pulled doubleheaders, attending both Sunday school and the adult religious services. The Catholic kids in the neighborhood were snooty and would taunt me, chanting that when I died I wouldn't go to heaven, and because I was Protestant I would have to settle for limbo.

I gave up God for baseball. The Triple A San Francisco Seals were my father's pride and joy. Lefty O'Doul managed the hometown team. Lefty had played in the big leagues and later would manage the San Diego Padres to a pennant in 1954, the year I graduated from high school.

My father's passion for the Seals was passed on down to me. Joe Sprinz, a former catcher who was the Seal's coach, formed two teams and slow-pitched for both sides. I was the top hitter on the best of the two teams. Sprinz's son had a crippled arm, but played the outfield better than most of the kids. He would catch the call in his gloved hand, drop the glove, transfer the ball to his good hand, and throw it back to the infield, without missing a beat.

Poetry and writing couldn't have been further from my mind. I spent my free time bouncing tennis balls off the concrete wall outside our flat on Page Street, living and breathing baseball, always looking for a pickup game. There were two baseball fields in Golden Gate Park, and you could always find a weekend game being played by one of the many semi-pro teams: Lucky Lager Beer, Moffit Manteca (a meatpacking plant), Horsetrader Ed's (used-car dealer), and others.

I remember the first time my father took me to a baseball game. It was the first time I had been inside Seals Stadium, which was located next to the old Southern Pacific Railroad tracks at Sixteenth and Bryant Street. I stood proudly at my father's side as he purchased two tickets. I was amazed at the hundreds of people walking through the gates to the park. Inside, it was circus-like excitement. Men selling programs. Hot dog and Coke concession stands. Men in colorful uniforms were walking up the aisles yelling. "Hot dogs, peanuts, Cracker Jacks."

I was amazed at how green the ball field was. The hometown Seals were on the field taking practice. Roy Nicely, a slick-fielding short-stop, was scooping up grounders as hitter after hitter sent the outfielders to the wall, many of the balls landing out of reach, into the bleachers. There they were, my hometown heroes hitting, throwing, yelling things like, "Hubba-hubba," dressed in their white striped uniforms. I don't think I've ever been happier in my life.

And then the umpire yelled, "Play ball," as the Seals took the field to loud applause. They were playing the rival Oakland Oaks. In the seventh inning, we stood up as the organist played "Take Me out to the Ball Game." I cheered when the crowd cheered, and jeered the umpire when the crowd yelled at him for making what they believed was the wrong call.

At the same time a distance developed between my father and

me, which reached its peak when he refused to take time off from work and take me to the annual father-son baseball game. The Seals were playing an exhibition game against the Cleveland Indians, and Bob Feller, the greatest pitcher of his time, was pitching the first three innings. My mother took me to the ball game, against my wishes. I was deeply embarrassed, the only boy in the ballpark with his mother.

As luck would have it Bob Feller drew my name from a raffle bowl, and I was called down to the ball field to have my picture taken for the evening edition of the old *News Call Bulletin*. I was the only boy in the picture standing without his father.

Family Man

Conceived in the womb
Of an indifferent marriage
I seemed to remind you of the anger
The failure of your own youth
Until childhood became a series
Of Gothic nightmares
An eighteen year sentence
At the Alamo
Your eyes a fixed bayonet
Your tongue a sharp dagger in
Adam's rib cage
Memories of your chasing me around
The dinner table
The sadistic hissing of the razor strap
Me a constant reminder of a depression
Era marriage taking you away from
Your world of music into a life
You wore like the ill-fitting clothes
On a hunchback
No room for me in your life
No room for a pacifist
I tried writing blood stained poems
To make you proud of me
Joined the military became
A government worker
Tried every trick in the book

To erase the scars you left like
A branding iron in my heart
At sixty-seven
Just one short year before
Your death
You were still into Truman
And MacArthur
The big war you couldn't be part of
Declared 4-F
Denied the manhood you sought
Left with a wife and son
To do battle with
Mother taking up the battle call
When you were too tired
To bear arms
No room for Buddha
The words clothed in death
Visions of that leather strap
Whispering in the air
Your eyes a German Luger
Taking aim from
The grave.

Polytechnic High School graduate, 1954

In my last year at the Pillar of Fire, something happened that would change my life forever. The regular teacher came down ill, and a substitute teacher was brought in to teach the class. On the first day of class, the new teacher handed out a class assignment. Each of us was given a picture of an old man sitting on a porch, staring into space. We were told to write about what we saw in the picture.

The next day the teacher handed back our class assignments, and I was surprised to receive an A. The teacher asked me to read the story in front of the class, but I was too shy. She read it to the class herself, and I could see the other kids were jealous. Later in private the teacher praised my writing skills. For the first time in my life I knew I was good at something.

I began spending a lot of time at the branch library on Page Street, reading the works of Jack London. I had a vague idea that I wanted to be a writer, but poetry wasn't part of the equation.

I enrolled at Polytechnic High School in 1950. My sister was a year ahead of me and was an honor student. I was expected to be like my sister, but I openly rebelled and made no effort to achieve anything more than a passing grade. This frustrated my teachers, many of whom had taught my sister in their classrooms.

I took pride in becoming the class clown. My crowning achievement was the day Mr. Lombardi, my English teacher, called me to the front of the room to read a book report. When I declined Mr. Lombardi said, "We're waiting for you."

"Fraid not," I said.

"Fraid you're going to be fraid to look at your report card," Mr. Lombardi responded.

I replied, "Mr. Lombardi, that's a double negative. I would think an English teacher would know better," This earned me a week in detention.

I associated with a gang of rough kids. We cut class, stole hubcaps from cars, shoplifted, and hung out at Ocean Beach trying to make it with the girls. None of us did.

The Korean War was on everyone's mind. We talked big about how we'd kick butt, but deep down we were afraid about the possibility of dying.

At home, my parents were still fighting. My mother wanted a divorce, but stayed married for the sake of my sister and me. My father's health was failing from smoking two packs of Pall Mall cigarettes a day, and my mother was forced to take in children to help make ends meet.

By now I had become acquainted with the works of Ernest Hemingway and F. Scott Fitzgerald and was pretty sure I wanted to be a writer, but lacked confidence in my English skills.

After graduation I bummed around for two months, working for a short period of time at the old Crystal Palace parking lot before

Lackland Air Force Base. 1954

joining the air force. On September 3, 1954, I reported to the air force recruiting station and was accepted for active duty. My military days were not happy ones. The day I arrived at boot camp, I was taken to a processing center and asked what my religion was. I replied Protestant. I was asked what denomination I was, and again I answered Protestant. I had no idea what "denomination" meant. To me there were only Catholics, Protestants, and Jews.

The sergeant felt I was being a wiseass and asked again what denomination I was, and I replied in the same manner. I was escorted to the barracks and told to strip down to my shorts and made to sit on a chair in the middle of the room, where the sergeant and a corporal used me for batting practice.

My dislike for the military and what it represented was branded into me by the drill instructor (DI). It took over forty years to write about my experiences, in a small book of poems titled *This Land Is Not My Land*. The book later won a Pen National Josephine Miles Award for Excellence in Literature.

Lackland Air Force Base Poem

The DI
Took us on a field exercise
Bagged a rabbit
Took out his survival knife
And slit it up the middle
Sliding his free hand inside
Coming out with its innards
Drank from the blood saying
It would make men of us
As two three others jumped in
While others screamed in joy
Or agony
One boy leaving his breakfast
On the ground
We wore the smell of death

Like a whore's sweet perfume
The day we graduated
Accepting honors at the
Company parade ground

After completing boot camp, I was assigned to Albrook Air Force
Base, Panama, where I played on the baseball team until I injured my
leg. As a result, I was assigned to the Air Police Unit, pulling guard
duty at remote jungle posts of no strategic military value.

My first year in Panama, the Panamanian president was gunned
down at the racetrack. There were three classes in Panama. The rich
people frequented the gambling casino at the Hilton Hotel. The
middle class comprised mainly Chinese immigrants who owned
the shops and small restaurants. The majority belonged to the lower
class, who lived in squalor and poverty in downtown Panama.

Memories

Panama City
Could have been any
Slum city in America
Run by corrupt police
And politicians
But when you add the
American troops
Sent there to safeguard
The people
It was worse than any slum
You might imagine
Taxi drivers taking you
To a donkey show
Or to homes of young whores
While less than ten miles away
In the American Canal Zone
It's home town U.S.A.
The Governor's Ball
U.S. Civilian police
White skinned women

Sipping coffee and tea
Armed forces tv selling the
American dream

It was while serving in Panama that I became disillusioned with the American system. Panamanian canal workers, who performed the same work as their American counterparts, were paid less than half the pay. In the American-controlled Canal Zone, the U.S. governor refused to allow the Panamanian flag to fly along-side the flag of the United States. Elections were rigged, and ballot boxes were found floating in the canal.

The Joseph McCarthy era, the struggle for civil rights, the treatment of the American Indian, and the Vietnam War all became fodder for rebellion, resulting in scores of scathing political poems.

In February 1958, I was discharged from the military and returned home to discover the Beat generation. I found a part-time night job working at the post office and attended day classes at City College of San Francisco (CCSF). I began reading the works of Steinbeck, Hesse, and Camus and became interested in poetry after discovering Ginsberg and Ferlinghetti and other Beat poets and writers. The GI Bill and the part-time job at the post office allowed me to pursue college prep courses. I graduated from CCSF in 1960, and in 1962 received a B.A. degree in sociology from San Francisco State College.

Lawrence Ferlinghetti and A.D. at the Abandoned Planet Bookstore, SF 1990s. Photographer unknown.

While attending college, I spent my nights in North Beach, spending long hours at City Lights Bookstore browsing through underground magazines. It was here that I discovered Ferlinghetti's *Coney Island of the Mind*, Patchen's *Love Poems*, Corso's *Gasoline*, Ginsberg's *Howl*, and other poets and poems that would influence me.

I drank at Vesuvio's Bar and hung out at Mike's Pool

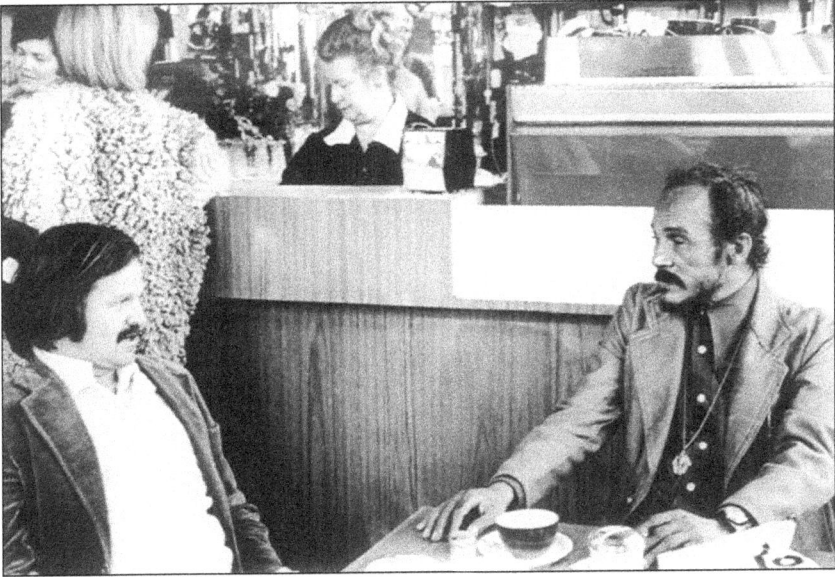

With Bob Kaufman (right), North Beach, SF. 1976. Photo by Richard Morris.

Hall and several watering holes on upper Grant Avenue. My favorite hangout was The Place, where Jack Spicer presided over "Blabbermouth Night," an occasion for poets and philosophers to get up and speak on any topic that came to their minds. I frequently saw Bob Kaufman sitting at one of the tables talking, drinking wine, and smoking grass, and Richard Brautigan walking down the street handing out xerox copies of his poems.

I frequented the Coffee Gallery and Gino and Carlo's bar, where I frequently saw Jack Spicer and Brautigan, and once shot pool with the late Janis Joplin.

I ate at Woy Loy Goys, a downstairs Chinese restaurant that served a low-price meal of Chinese greens and rice, tea, and a pork roll. My favorite restaurant, however, was Sam Woo's whose waiter, Edsel Ford, had the sharpest tongue in town. You had to pass through a butcher shop and walk upstairs to eat, and the food was brought up to you in a dumbwaiter.

It was in North Beach that I met Kaufman, Micheline, Corso, and Ferlinghetti.

In the sixties and early seventies I worked at a variety of conventional jobs while earning a B.A. degree from San Francisco State College, as it was then known. My poetry frequently appeared in small literary magazines, and in 1970 my first book of poems, *Carmel Clowns*, was published by Atom Mind Press.

Carmel Clowns

Carmel clowns walk the street
Hippies try hard but can't look beat
Normal Norm plays trick or treat while
The Universe grows gargoyle feet

Discovering North Beach opened a new life for me. I don't go there much anymore, maybe two or three times a year. Like everything else, it has changed.

While attending college and working at the post office, I met Ernie Gaines, who was attending Stanford University and aspiring to be a writer. While sorting mail we discussed writing, and I sensed even then that he would be successful. I was right. Gaines went on to write *The Autobiography of Miss Jane Pittman* and several other outstanding novels.

After graduating from San Francisco State in 1962, I enrolled in two postgraduate creative writing classes: "Introduction to Creative Writing" and "The Art of Short Story Writing."

My decision to take these classes was probably influenced by the reputation of the State Poetry Center. The center featured poet lecturers like Charles Olson and Marianne Moore. Mark Harris was also part of the program, but things were changing.

I dropped out of the short-story writing class after the instructor offered no rebuttal to a young man's criticism that F. Scott Fitzgerald's metaphors were outdated. The "Introduction to Creative Writing" course was even worse. The instructor didn't like Jack Kerouac, whose work he described as "pretentious and self-indulgent." The instructor told the class that Kerouac was not a "legitimate" writer and strongly discouraged anyone from using Kerouac's writing style.

I dropped the class in record time.

The job at the post office was beginning to take its toll. It wasn't so much the work (which was bad enough), but the brain-dead supervisors who abused their authority. After work I would go across the street to the corner bar and drink the remaining hours away. The experience is described in a poem I wrote.

Post Office Poem

After my shift at the post office
I'd stop for a drink at the corner bar
And chat with Carl the German bartender
But mostly I'd just sit and listen
To the jukebox
I remember this one guy who came
In every night
Who would play Ray Charles
BORN TO LOSE
And I'd order another drink
Watching the clock wind down
Bone-ass tired from sorting
Thousands of letters and parcels
Fingers numb from stuffing them
Into pigeon holes or sacks
Smelling of sweat and death
I kept drinking until I felt good
Or ran out of money or both
Riding the "14" Mission bus home
With other people like me
Who stared straight ahead
Out the window
Or down at their feet
Night shift people
Who couldn't do a nine-to-five
And when I got off the bus
I made my way up those
Long six blocks
To my apartment and poured
Myself a drink
Turned on the hi-fi
Plopped my tired ass
Down on the bed
Let Billie Holiday sing
Me to sleep

I quit the post office to accept a full-time job as a juvenile probation officer in Modesto. I was assigned a caseload of over two hundred juvenile delinquents and quit less than five months later. I worked at several government jobs until I quit work in 1973 to devote my full time to writing.

The sixties and seventies were an exciting time for me. I met and hung out with post-beat poets Kell Robertson and Wayne Miller and small-press veterans like Ben Hiatt. I was the first paid feature reader at the Old Coffee Gallery, receiving five dollars and all the beer I could drink. I read my work with Kaufman and Micheline at a "street poets" reading at U.C. Berkeley Extension, and later with Kaufman, DiPrima, Ferlinghetti, Joane Kyger, and others at the Little Fox Theater on Broadway Street.

I gave a lot of readings during the seventies, reading on benefit bills with such distinguished poets as Robert Hass and the late Josephine Miles. I began writing fiction again, submitting my work to both slick magazines and underground newspapers like the old Berkeley Barb. I sold two short stories to Easy Rider magazine for $175 each, and several prose pieces to the *Berkeley Barb*.

North Beach maintained its excitement and reputation as a home for poets and writers all the way through the seventies, but it was the late fifties and sixties that shaped my life. The Co-existence Bagel Shop, where Kaufman hung out, was a lively meeting place for poets, painters, and philosophers. It was here that Kaufman wrote on the wall, "Adoph Hitler tired of burning Jews and fooling around with Eva Braun moved to North Beach and became a cop." This earned Kaufman the special attention of the San Francisco police, who frequently arrested him and took him to the Old Kearney Street, Hall of Justice, where he was subjected to beatings.

North Beach was a place where blacks and whites freely hung out together. Marijuana and wine were plentiful, and I spent many nights at Big Daddy Nord's pad, located near the old produce district, where bongo and conga drums played day and night. America was undergoing a revolution, and North Beach and New York's Greenwich Village were the focal points. By the sixties most of the Beats had left North Beach. But the post-Beat poets would keep the tradition alive for another twenty years.

I felt privileged to have lived through two of the most exciting periods of our time, the Beat era and the hippie generation. I over-lapped into both. LSD was the choice of drugs in the Haight-Ashbury. Ken Kesey and his Merry Pranksters frequently appeared in the Haight, wearing the colors of the U.S. flag. Psychedelic shops were the rule and not the exception. Carlos Santana and Janis Joplin and the Grateful Dead were just a few of the bands that became famous.

The year 1965 brought with it the full horror of the Vietnam conflict. The antiwar movement grew in numbers, and it was during this era that one of my first political poems was published.

Reflections

turned in the television set
down the hall
turned on the societal ball
wall street ticker-tape parade
for moon men
broadway go-go girls doing the swim
burned children crying in my ear
the president playing on my fears
facts and figures more government lies
another commercial another young boy dies
heroism found in Vietnam fields
hospital costs rising according
To blue shield
flowers grow and bloom
funeral horses strangle on gargoyle plumes
baby crying in the background
head so fucked up can't make a sound
latest love lays naked in bed
only one damn thing going on inside
her head

In 1976 the first Human-Be-In was held at Golden Gate Park. I was there with one hundred thousand other people. There were free drugs. Free music. Free sex. It was a sight to behold.

The Haight-Ashbury became the new Bohemia. A loose-knit coalition sprang up, consisting of Beats who were able to make the transition and new-age hippies. Ginsberg was most at home in the hippie era, flourishing as a sort of half-king, half-guru spokesman for the new generation.

The Human-Be-In brought together the Beats, poets radical politicians, and a large number of rock groups like the Grateful Dead and Big Brother and the Holding Company. I saw Tim Leary, for the first time, at the bandstand playing with small children. For twenty-four hours we held the world in the palm of our hands.

The Beats, perhaps not willingly, passed on the baton to the post-Beat poets of North Beach: Wayne Miller, Dan Propper, George Tsongas, Janice Blue, David Plumb, Gene Ruggles, Kaye McDonough, Janice Blue, Kell Roberston and myself were regulars in North Beach. Poetry readings were everywhere. The bars may have changed their names, but they were still frequented by poets, artists and writers.

A.D. and Paddy O'Sullivan North Beach, SF. 1976. Photo by Richard Morris.

Paddy O'sullivan and Bob Kaufman were still around, and Ferlinghetti continued his presence at City Light Bookstore. Paddy was a central character in the Beat era, a minor poet who supported himself by hawking a pocket-sized book of his poems titled *Weep Not My Children*. Paddy would stand on the corner dressed in a purple cape, plumed hat, and high boots, with shoulder-length hair. A modern-day cavalier, he greeted female tourists with a courteous bow and a kiss on the hand.

However, it was Bob Kaufman who stood above the other poets. A hipster among the hip. A Black Jesus of the fifties. The first time I saw Kaufman read his poetry he was dressed in a corduroy jacket and beret and sporting a goatee, and I remember thinking he looked more like a Greenwich Village artist than a poet.

Kaufman made an immediate impression on me. He was a giant among the surrealist poets, and his imagery was more profound and humorous than the Beat poets who later gained fame. Kaufman could recite T. S. Eliot's *Love Song of J. Alfred Prufrock* by heart, as he could the works of several other major poets. He loved jazz and knew Charlie Parker, Mingus, and Lester Young. Kaufman had taken a vow of silence after the assassination of President Kennedy. A vow he kept until the Vietnam War ended.

The night kaufman officially broke his vow of silence, I was at Spec's bar, waiting on a ride to party being hosted by Miriam Pachen, when Kaufman entered and began a half-hour non stop recitation of poems of Eliot, Blake, Pound and others. I didn't go to the party that night. I was so moved that I stayed behind and wrote a poem for Kaufman on cocktail napkins. The poem hung in a glass case outside Spec's for over fifteen years. Even today Bob Kaufman remains very much on my mind, as evidenced by this poem I wrote for him in 1996, ten years after his death.

On the Anniversary of the Death of Bob Kaufman

The hollow sockets that once
Housed your eyes invade
My thoughts tonight
As blurred images of the skull
Play my nerve ends like
A skilled violinist
How is it out there among
The stars?
Are poets issued wings?

I had a dream last night
I saw you driving across
The face of the moon

Picking up astral speed
As you reached a crater where
God stood chatting with Jesus

He had a cold beer in his hand
Resting next to a lamp post
Looking like Bogart back from
A night on the town

Just before I woke up
I thought I saw you parachuting
Toward earth
Jesus riding your coat-tails

Another poet who influenced me was Jack Micheline, Jack was born in the Bronx and walked the streets with Jack Kerouac, who wrote an introduction for Micheline's first book *River of Red Wine*, Jack's first book of poems.

It's easy for me to identify with Micheline. His work speaks to and addresses the down and out, the misfits of society: the dopers, hookers, homosexuals, and destitute population spurned by the majority of society. We went to the track together, read on the same poetry bill, and got drunk in the same bars. It was from listening to Micheline read and his rapport with the audience that I developed my own reading style.

Poem for Jack Micheline

this poem is for you
and the streets you have walked
from San Francisco to New York and back
you who have traveled the unmarked grave
that stretches like a long line of coffins
floating across the sewers of America
heading East and West where poets who
never had a chance grasped for
Kerouac's dream buried beneath
an ocean of tears where
stone faced politicians suck
the bones to the marrow feeding
on the scraps of the poor boy poet
who like you carry
their visions like diamonds
in the sky

Hanging out with small-press editors and publishers like Kell Robertson and Ben Hiatt, I became interested in publishing.

Ed Lipman and A.D. -1976 - Second Coming Party in celebration of the publication of the 1976 California Bicentennial Poetry Anthology - Photo by Bil Paul

Robertson, myself, and Grover Lewis, a writer from *Rolling Stone* magazine, would get drunk and close down the bars in North Beach.

In 1972 I began publishing *Second Coming*, a literary journal that later expanded into a book publisher producing over twenty-two books and anthologies.

The small presses in the sixties and seventies provided an environment where a person could experience life firsthand. I found myself in the company of people committed not only to literature but equally to social justice. The alternative presses were publishing innovative and revolutionary literature. Some of the more outrageous small-press magazines (*Fuck You* and *Willie*) found themselves threatened with censorship by the postal authorities. The magazine *Willie* was edited by a poet who called himself Willie Gobblecunt, not exactly endearing himself to the postal authorities.

I became identified with the Meat poets. The Meat poets were so named because they wrote about the meat-and-potato issues of the day. Everything on planet earth constituted poetry: fucking, cursing, drugs, race, prison. The movement was led by Charles

A.D. in 1975

Bukowski, whose intent was to "loosen" the language of poetry. Form was secondary to content. Rhythm and meter, as we know, was scorned and discarded.

The first issue of *Second Coming* was slick in appearance and saddle-stitched, featuring mostly small-press veteran poets. The issue was timeless (by design), with no cover date, copy-right, or issue date.

Second Coming was open to all schools of poetry and frequently published poems that had first appeared elsewhere. The second issue was 7" by 8½". I wanted it to be different and unique, while at the same time setting the tone of the magazine. This issue saw the addition of artwork as I tried to match the written word to the visual. Later issues included photography, primarily by Mark Green and Bill Paul.

The third issue was 8¼" by 11¼". I became more involved in the production of the magazine. The first two years of the *SC* saw me and a few friends collating the issues, and I helped bind one of the issues, thanks to a friend of mine who worked at a local print shop. As time passed grant money from the Coordinating Council of Literary Magazines (CCLM) and the National Endowment for the Arts (NEA) allowed me to expand the print run and turn *Second Coming* from a saddle-stitched magazine into a slick, perfect-bound literary journal.

Second Coming is frequently referred to as a Beat publication, but the truth is that the magazine published many writers of importance outside the Beat movement. It was multicultural before the word became popular. The only thing I insisted on was that the writing be vibrant.

From 1975 to 1980 I worked as an editor-writer for the Neighborhood Arts Program at the San Francisco Art Commission, spending fifty percent of my time on *Second Coming* projects, which included teaching in two public schools and organizing poetry and music events. The crowning achievement of my years at the Art Commission was the 1980 Poets and Music Festival sponsored by *Second Coming*, a seven-day, three-county poetry and music festival honoring the poet Josephine Miles and the blues great John Lee Hooker.

I'm proud of the poetry and music events *Second Coming* sponsored, and the special literary projects over a seventeen-year period. Projects like the special Charles Bukowski issue, an anthology of New Zealand poetry, the California bicentennial poets anthology, and the anthology of San Francisco poets, and several books of poetry by minority and prison poets. It was through *Second Coming* that I met Charles Bukowski, whom I went on to enjoy a seventeen-year friendship with.

During this time I became a board member of the Committee of Small Magazine Editors and Publishers (COSMEP), serving two consecutive terms on the board before resigning in 1977 for personal reasons. Later, with the late Noel Peattie, I helped create Western Independent Publishers (WIP), which is no longer in existence.

During the seventies my own work flourished. The year 1977 saw three books of poems published, including *North Beach Poems*. At the same time *Second Coming* was at the height of its publishing efforts. As part of *Second Coming's* commitment to political justice, I frequently participated in the Folsom Prison Writers' Workshop. The following poem touches on my experience.

Folsom Prison

At Folsom Prison
The guards joke and laugh
As they have me empty
My pockets inside out
Taking everything from me
Leaving me with only my note book
And a handful of poems
The guard in the watch tower
Watching the prisoners in
The court yard below
His hi-powered rifle
At the ready.

The warden distrustful
Maybe even fearful
Stations a guard outside
The small room where
The poetry workshop is held
The sharing of words
Barely begins when
I look outside the window
See a bird light on top
Of the prison wall
Looking East then West
Before spreading its wings
And flying North
Free as free was meant to be
As I turn my attention
To the guard in the back
Of the room
Hiding behind dark shades
Looking more the outlaw
Than the law

The Art Commission job ended in 1980, and I bummed around on unemployment for six months before survival dictated my taking a job as a security guard at Saint Francis Hospital in San Francisco. The job was living hell. I worked the midnight shift and developed insomnia and had little energy to write. *Second Coming* began to appear less frequently.

In 1984 the San Francisco Arts and Letters Foundation presented me with a cash award in recognition of my "contribution to small press Literature." Other honors followed: a song poem of mine being performed at Tully Hall, NYC; and in 2009 Pen Oakland presenting me with a Lifetime Achievement Award.

I suffered a severe neck injury in 1988 and was unable to work for nearly two years. *Second Coming* ceased publishing a short year later.

In 1990 Alpha Beat Press published a small chapbook, *In Memoriam*. A month later I accepted a full-time job as a equal opportunity specialist for the U.S. Department of Education, Office for Civil Rights, investigating discrimination against minorities,

A.D. in Sacramento, CA 1998. Photo by Roger Langton

women and the disabled. The job was both demanding and stressful, made worse by incompetent managers who were more concerned with closing cases and earning fat bonuses than with ensuring a person's civil rights. Both my writing and health suffered.

In April 1995, I took an early retirement, which has allowed me the freedom to write full-time. I found my writing immediately rejuvenated. In the two years following my retirement. I had several chapbooks of poetry published, and my first prose book, *The Charles Bukowski/Second Coming Years*, was published by Beat Scene, and later republished in an expanded version (*The Holy Grail: Charles Bukowski and the Second Coming Years*) by Dustbooks. My work has being translated into nine languages, and in 2010 BOS Press published a 369 page book of my selected poems: *Downing Lik Li Po in a River Red Wine*.

The years have passed much too quickly, but I recorded the times, both good and bad, in poems and short stories. How I managed to survive all these years is something only the gods know. I've been in situations and places where I could have been killed, and once nearly was.

While I never lived on the streets, I lived on the edge. I have known and associated with people from all walks of life. When someone says that I'm a poet, I smile. I'm not a prophet or a shaman, but more a caretaker who writes down what he has observed and lived.

A.D.'s mother in the 1970s

My mother died in 1990. I made peace with her the year before her death.

Remembering My Mother

After the funeral
We gathered at my sister's home
Sharing memories
When I looked through one of my
Mother's family photo albums
And there she was back in
1944
During the war
She and auntie working for
The Red Cross
Stuffing boxes of cigarettes
And chocolates for our boys overseas
She was young and pretty
Had a smile on her face

And as I turned the pages
Life became a blur
A butcher knife in my hand
As I headed down the road
Of my childhood
One last time
Achieving in death what
Was never possible in life
Memories from the past
Hers/Mine
The blood thick as bread crust

My one regret is that I never had the opportunity for closure with my father.

Poetry and writing have kept me going throughout the years. It's been the wife and children I've never had. I've published over fifty books and chapbooks of poetry and prose, and have had poems published in well over a thousand literary magazines and anthologies.

I've given countless readings, and made lifelong friends. None of this would have been possible if I hadn't found the magic of poetry. However, there is no substitute for how you live your life. It's been good meeting the people I have met. It's been good hearing my work praised by poets and writers like Studs Terkel, Herbert Gold, Jack Micheline, Colin Wilson, Alvah Bessie (one of the Hollywood Ten who went to prison during the Senator McCarthy witchhunt era, "House on Un-American Activities Committee"), Charles Bukowski, and others whom I deeply respect.

I believe that in the long run my poems and prose will tell you most about who I am. As I said, my life and poetry can't be separated. I get up in the morning, have a cup of coffee and read the paper, spend a couple hours at the computer, pick up the mail at the post office, take a long hour walk, return home, listen to my jazz records, put in another few hours of writing, and then it's time to go to bed and get up in the morning and start all over again.

That's what life is pretty much about. The growing up, the learning, the wild years, the mellowing, the settling into a routine, and then one day it's over.

I'm lucky to have Brown University house my archives and the archives of *Second Coming*. I've gotten back to jazz again. As I write this, I'm listening to Miles Davis recorded in San Francisco at the Black Hawk in 1963. I was there the night he performed. It's a night I'll always remember.

I have a tape of Patchen reading his poetry to jazz. Miles Davis and Kenneth Patchen and Billie Holiday have seen me through many a lonely night.

Looking out at this great city of San Francisco, I say that's enough. Writing poetry has helped keep lady death from my door. The demons are still there inside me, but I no longer let them control me.

I don't think any one man's life is really that important, but what he does with it and leaves behind is.

I hope I have earned more good karma than bad karma points. I hope in the end I can look death in the face and say that I've played the game honestly and that I never sold my integrity. In the end integrity is all a writer has. Sell your integrity and you've sold your soul to the devil.

It's How You Look at It

Sitting here alone as
I've grown accustomed
Listening to Billie Holiday
Pounding the computer keyboard
Trying to make a little magic
Jack Daniels racing through
My veins
Having just returned from
A book party celebrating
The life of Bob Kaufman
Gone like so many others
An army of poets sitting
On my bookshelf
T. S. Eliot playing
The banker
William Carlos Williams
Suturing wounds

Ferlinghetti in his navy suit
Kaufman walking the streets
Of New York singing his magic
To Charlie Parker
Blake playing cards with God
Lorca playing Russian roulette
Gary Snyder building word bridges
And suddenly I'm not alone anymore
The words falling like
Hard rain.

SAN FRANCISCO POEMS

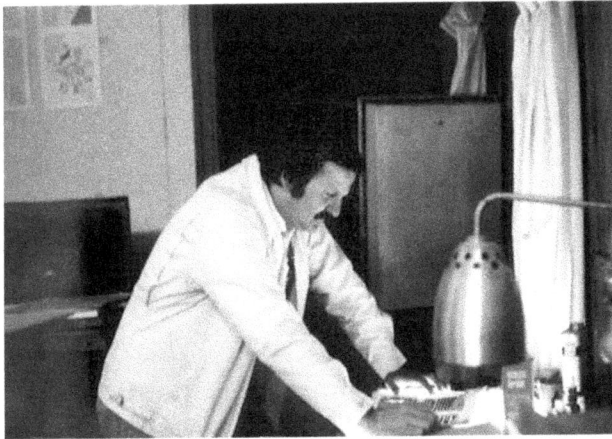

A.D. Winans. Photo by Wilfredo Castano.

I AM SAN FRANCISCO

I have witnessed the waterfront decay
the ships disappear
the piers given over to tourists
and sunbathing sea lions

Gone the Haight Theater
in the old Haight Ashbury
where as a kid I paid a dime to see
two movies a serial and a newsreel

Gone the old Embassy Theater
on Market Street where
they spun the Wheel of Fortune
playing Ten-O-Win
with a busty female usherette shouting
"In the Balcony, 1-2-3-4 Silver Dollars"
her breasts bouncing in unison
with each coin that hit the tray

the old Fox and Paramount Theaters
now ghostly memories
the old Market Street porno house
boarded down
the Crystal Palace market
Mc Farland's Fudge Shop
and Merrill's Drug Store gone

Gone the old Hoffbrau house
on Market Street
Breen's on Third Street
with the world's best Martini

Gone I. Magnin's Department Store
and the old City of Paris
where as a child I thrilled
at the sight of the giant Christmas tree
and who can forget The Emporium
its indoor ice-skating rink

and a Santa Claus workshop
the rooftop garden where
rides included a Ferris wheel
a small roller coaster
and a train for children to ride

Gone the North Beach Beat hangouts:
"The Place The Co-existence Bagel Shop
and the old Coffee Gallery" where
Janice Joplin sang as an unknown
gone the old Barbary Coast where
as a teenager I tried to sneak into a bar
to catch a glimpse of a naked female dancer
long before Carol Doda
and topless and bottomless bars

gone the old Black Hawk where
I saw Miles Davis play
Lenny Bruce and the old Purple Onion
fading memories like
Play Land at the beach
and the old burlesque house
in the Mission
gone the way of trolley car tokens
Fleer's Double Bubble Gum
and the Sutro baths

Third and Howard Street
the old skid row given a face-lift
the new skid row between
Sixth and Seventh Streets
home to drug dealers and alcoholics
an open festering wound
the city fathers ignore

Martini's now an old people's drink
Whiskey Sours just a memory
the Waterfront dives that served
Seamen and Long Shoremen replaced
by new movie complexes and parking lots

The Mission once home of the Irish
has gone Latino
North Beach is moving
from Italian to Asian

The Greeks long ago moved to Burlingame
and no one knows what happened
to the American Indian
and the bar they frequented
on Valencia Street
and yet the city remains a magical
living breathing theater
of eccentric characters
that go back to Emperor Norton

You can still get a reasonably priced drink
at the 3300 Club in the Mission
or if you can afford it
go to the Top of the Mark
for a $13 hot chocolate drink with
a shot of Stolly Vodka and Southern Comfort
and enjoy one of the most beautiful views
in the world
or on a hot summer afternoon enjoy
an ice cream at Mitchell's on San Jose Avenue
where my father took the family
for an after-dinner treat

You can still sun yourself
at Washington Square Park
watch young lovers lying on the grass
old men feeding pigeons
or walk the streets of Noe Valley
once a blue-collar neighborhood
now a Yuppie paradise
see young mothers with kids in strollers
eye women joggers
admire a dog sitting outside
Martha's Coffee Shop
faithfully waiting with pleading eyes

for table scraps from its owner
I'm a Giants baseball fan

and a lifetime 49ers football addict
my heart still bleeds over the loss
of Seal's Stadium and the old time
San Francisco Seals

I am the possessor
of framed achievement awards
and a baseball trophy from Panama where
I played a decent outfield

I am the only word-slinger
in a working class family
I am a ghost lost
in poetry books struggling to find
the right words to a hit song
like my idol Hank Williams Sr

I am at war with my shadow
who shamelessly stalks me
I survived my apartment fire
to reestablish family ties
long buried in quicksand

my niece my nephew my great nephews
and great niece share my blood
a mixture of white and Mexican roots

my father's ghost walks my dreams
stares out the window of my soul
like he stared out the living room window
the year before his death
my mother sitting at the dinner table
serving meat loaf and mashed potatoes
the air heavy as an anchor dragging
the ocean floor

I am San Francisco.

CITY POET

Once addiction sets in
There is no stopping it
You become a serial killer
Attacking the keyboard at will
Your mind works in shifts
Strange creatures live inside your head
Show no mercy
Give no ground
Force your fingers to do their bidding
Writing down their thoughts
In your loose-leaf notebook

The city is your slaughterhouse
Like a wife it accommodates your moods
Doesn't seem to mind
You giving her a bad name
You walk her streets a hungry vampire
Lapping up your own blood
On nights when blood transfusions
Are not enough

GOING BACK IN TIME

I was looking at my scrapbook the other night
while listening to an old Dylan record
and there I was in my youth
traveling from California to Arizona
and places further west
heading in so many directions
It was like being lost in the trick mirrors
at the old Fun House at Ocean Beach
and there were the young women
then young girls with free flowing spirits
who gave their minds and bodies
at the slightest invitation
and nights too lying alone in tangled sleep
feeling like a deer caught in barbed wire
or sitting hunched-over cold and disheveled
at the local Greyhound bus station
fighting off the eyes of leering men
who preferred boys to women
now seventy-two and counting
I realize I was there and back so fast
like a train running out of track
returning home carrying my life
in a Knapp-sack
the days the months the years
hung out to dry
like you mother's washing
on a frail clothesline

THE WRONG SIDE OF TOWN

cop's flashlight intruding on my thoughts
nightstick rapping on my window
demanding to know what I'm doing out
at this ungodly hour
ordered out of car frisked
and taken downtown for questioning
police suspicious why a white boy
would be listening to a tape ·
of a black musician
in a respectable part of town

SATURDAY NIGHT SPECIAL

No need to go out to a movie
More than enough action right
Here at home
Sirens wailing in the night
Police helicopter circling above
Searchlight igniting the sky

Shadow like figure leaps over fence
Like a skilled track hurdler
Dogs barking faces peering out the window
Neighbors hugging the night air
Like a chilled lover shivering
In anticipation

Intruder frozen in spotlight
Drops flat to the ground
Looking like a dead man
Laid out beneath a sea of stars

SATURDAY NIGHT HAPPENINGS

The air has that stale cigarette smell
Rancid as spoiled meat
The men in blue work the crime scene
Laying down yellow tape and chalk lines
That circle the corpse riddled with bullets

The people pushed back behind the barrier
Mill around like autograph seekers
Waiting on a matinee idol
Go home the mustached cop says
Bullhorn in hand
Go home, no story here
Go home
One more drive-by shooting
One more Saturday night death
Waiting on a Sunday morning headline
Go home
        No story here
Go home
        No story here

REMEMBERING

how I used to get into
the neighborhood movie show
for a dime
back when I was a child
growing up in the Haight Ashbury
before the Hippie era
or down on Market Street
at the Embassy Theater where
they spun the Wheel of Fortune
playing ten-o-win
yelling out the lucky winner
as a busty female usher raced
up the aisle shouting:
"In the balcony,
1-2-3-4 silver dollars"
her breasts bouncing in unison
with the dropping of each silver coin
only fading memories now
gone like the trolley car tokens
like Fleer's Double Bubble gum
Play land at the Beach
and the Sutro hot baths
fragments out of reach
like an aging gypsy woman
reading tea leaves
and finding a death note
in the hands of a faceless conductor
found lifeless three blocks short
of the end of the line

COCAINE ANNIE

cocaine Annie biker queen
making love to the jukebox machine
hands caress well-curved hips
eyes cowboy at the bar
digs her boots into the floor
wonders if he's worth a ride
tugs at her black leather jacket
slides hands down jean clad legs
heads out the door
opts for her Harley
gunning the engine
heading down highway 101
all the man she needs
vibrating between
her well-shaped legs

SOUTH OF MARKET

You can see from
The look in his eyes
The scar on his face that
He's someone you don't want
To mess with

His eyes survey the scene
Like a periscope
He's a two-bit thug
Looking for action
An old time beat cop
Looking for a head to bash
He's Boston Blackie and Al Capone
Rolled into one

His women are mean and lean
Bred on the S&M scene
With tattooed flesh and black mesh
They walk the seedy side of town
Looking to do the last waltz with you
In a back alley at South of Market
Or in a basement dungeon
It's all the same
All part of the game
Doing a tap dance on your spine
Looking dead serious
Like a sumo wrestler
Sizing you up for the kill

CHINATOWN SWEAT SHOP

You see them coming
but never going
Working l4-l6 hour shifts
6-7 days a week

I imagine the sewing machines
humming, "A stitch in time
saves nine."
You see them coming
but never going

I imagine the madam's eyes
An executioner in disguise
Watching waiting as
The universe grinds them into oblivion

d.a.LEVY WAS DEAD RIGHT

d.a. Levy was dead right
nothing changes
the trees shed their leaves like
a summer TV special
the undertaker unceremously
goes about his business
the walls hide messages
like greedy hoarders
the doorbell rings
the telephone rings nothing changes
it is all the same

the old man thinks of death
the young man thinks of riches
poets have become
exotic merchants of death

butterflies are beautiful
they have no desire
to fly to the moon
like the poet Kaufman said
"poets don't sneak into zoos
and talk to tigers anymore"

it's perfectly all right
to cast the first stone
if you have more than
the other person

nothing changes
the boxing matches
the bullfights go on
like a tired tongue resting between
the legs of a bored woman

the truth is that d.a. Levy was right
"sum people just can not beat the system
and poets can't even pretend
they are beating the system"

FOR JAMIE

Sitting alone at
The Lost and Found Bar
Here in North Beach
Dark skin centuries removed
From the present
Tapping your fingers
To the late afternoon music
Coming from the jukebox

No longer able to play
Your saxophone
Now sitting alone like you
Forgotten in a downtown
Pawnshop
Tagged for a quick sale

Someone puts a dollar
In the jukebox
And Billie Holiday
Sings softly in your ear
Bringing an instant smile
To your face

A lighthouse beam
Dividing the thin line
Between sanity
And madness

This is your turf
Your veins burning
With the energy of life
Long lines of images
Haunting the early afternoon
Hours

Bronzed warrior of old
Sitting here
At the Lost and Found Bar
The beat forever going on

THE BLACK HAWK 1963

The old Black Hawk booked
The best jazz musicians of its day
Diz, Getz, Miles Davis
Just to name a few

I went there but twice
Once with the poet Jack Micheline
Once with a young Latina girl
To see Miles Davis blow his magic

Forced to sit in the Teenage section
Because she was only seventeen
Sipping on a coke
High on the high note
Smoke curling around the room
In long lingering lazy circles

Sweet sax Smooth gin tonic
My hand on warm thigh
Feeling high Feeling cool
Be-bop rhythms dancing inside
My soul

JAZZ ANGEL

she sits alone in her small
hotel room above
the "222 Club"
in the heart of the Tenderloin
six months pregnant
forced to give head
for soup and bread
no heat one wash cloth
one yellow stained washbasin

hope bled dry
immigrant without visa or status
an illegal caught in a legal trap
feels the baby stir move inside her
Billie Holiday plays On jukebox
in bar below

she heads for the door
hears the night manager whisper "whore"
suspended in silence and grief
floats face down in the bowels
of the American dream

MEMORIES

No more jazz at the Black Hawk
No more jazz at the Cellar
No more jazz in the Fillmore
Just ghostly boarded-down doors
Gone the clinking of glasses
The waitress who always knew
When your glass was empty
Casting her spell on your nerve ends

The black female crooner
Hitting her notes like a midnight train
With its long wailing whistle
Her sultry smile imbedded in your skin
Long after the closing hour
Leaving you sweating
Like the first moments
After a wet dream

OLD WARRIOR OF NORTH BEACH

He walks the streets of North Beach
Like an old man
With eyes empty as a broken parking meter
Unemployable weighed down by the years
His mind heavy as an anchor dragging
The bottom of the ocean floor

Forgotten rebel playing old ballads
In the shipwreck of his heart
His mind destroyed by shock treatments
And one too many police batons

At night he dreams he is riding with Geronimo
Has imaginary conversations with Charlie Parker
Rides the ferry with Miles Davis
Getting off at Bourbon Street
To down a drink with Kerouac

He shares a cigarette with Charlie Chaplin
At the old Bijo Theater
Walks the battlefields with Walt Whitman
Rides the plains with Red Cloud
In search of the last buffalo
Walks the streets of North Beach
In search of the elusive ginger fish smell
Death a sightless chauffeur
Waiting like a concubine facing down another
Faceless John

OLD JOE

He sleeps in doorways
Or on park benches
Doesn't want to go
To a shelter
Not even when prodded
With the heavy weight
Of the beat cop's nightstick
Under threat of jail
He curls up in a fetal position
And closes his eyes
Trying to shut out memories of Vietnam
Nightmares that whirl inside his head
Like helicopter blades

The alcohol the drugs
The failed years gather like locusts
Inside the cranial guitar of his mind
Playing all night rhapsodies inside
His head

Warrior troubadour of Pharaoh origins
Pale spokesman of lost tribes
Masked as a homeless transient
Poet Prophet of beauty
And all its imperfections
Ravished by the streets
Kissed by angels
Left tired withered
Like an unattended Kansas
Grain field

FOR JACK MICHELINE

This poem is for you
And the city streets you walked
From San Francisco to New York
You who traveled the unmarked grave
That stretches like a long line of coffins
Floating across the sewers of America
Heading East and West
Where poets who never had a chance
Lived Kerouac's dream
Buried beneath an ocean of tears
Where solemn politicians
Suck the bones to the marrow
Feeding on the scraps of poor boy poets
Who like you carried their visions
Like diamonds in the sky

POEM FOR ALEXSEY DAYEN

the drums beat slowly
the angels march in sleep
like a Chinatown funeral march
a New Orleans jazz tribute
sending you off on a new voyage
like the Vikings of old

the drums beat slowly
echo loud across the universe where
Kaufman and Micheline await you
with drinks in hand

the drums beat slowly for
the Prince of New York and Moscow
the drums beat slowly serenade
the heartbeat of grieving friends
church bells toll in mourning
guitars play in the streets of Russia
wailing saxophones sing their song
in the streets of New York

your poems your children clothed
in memories, the dark clouds
a candle that can't be blown out

deep in the forest of the mind
flowers bloom forever and beyond
where friends wait to walk with you again

the drums will beat forever
my friend
in the heart in the brain
in the head where
poems embrace the dead

your eternal light
a butterfly spreads its wings
heaven bound
cosmic matter waiting
to be reborn

SAN FRANCISCO STREETS

I've walked these San Francisco streets
Like a crime photographer walks his beat
My eyes taking in her every movement
My brain storing real and imagined changes
In seventy years her changes have not eluded me
She is older now
More wrinkled and cranky
Much like me
But the two of us manage to get along
Like business partners looking after
Each other's interest
Market Street once a fashionable socialite
Now a gaudy whore
Mission Street once the home of the Irish
Now glossed over
Tough looking youths with dagger stares
Where you guard your wallet
Like a eunuch guards the harem door

You have to learn to give and take
You have to learn to adjust
The city is like a cup of strong coffee
Stir her enough
And the flavor floats to the top

I have walked these streets
In good condition
And broken down physique
Knowing there is no city
Like her in the world

She is like a pair
Of empty shoes
Sitting under the bed
With no feet big enough
To fill them

She is like a squirrel running through
The live wires of a utility pole
She is like the last bullet
In the executioner's gun
She is like a room full of poets
Crazed with their own conversation

She is like Billie Holiday
Drenched in sweat
She is like the face of God
All forgiving
In her insatiable lust
For life

THANK GOD FOR SMALL FAVORS

the night brings no pain
thank god for small favors
thank god for Billie Holiday
on the radio
crystal lying naked
on the bed beside me
not a muscle moving
where only hours ago
we had been grooving

outside in the alley
a cat marks its turf
more at home than
I've ever been

CITY HAPPENINGS

They're having a rumble
At Ellis and Eddy street
And the police are slow
To respond
You can see the rage
In the Chicano's eyes
Smell the fear in Whitey

The blacks are shucking and jiving
Rolling dice and placing bets
On winner and losers alike
The street whores move down
A block or two to ply their trade
One white One Asian One Spade

The cops arrive at last
Dispersing the players
Like bit actors auditioning
For a role in the big show

Small time punks gather themselves
Run for cover
Don't stop to look back
Head for the crack house
Biding their time
Like a stoned Jesus
Hung out to dry
On your mother's clothes line

POST OFFICE REFLECTION

After my shift at Rincon Annex
I'd stop off for a drink
At the corner bar and chat with
Carl the German bartender
But mostly I'd just sit and listen
To the jukebox
And I remember this one guy
Who came in every night
And played Ray Charle's
"Born to Lose"
And I'd order another drink
And watch the clock tick down
Bone-ass tired
From sorting thousands of letters
My fingers numb from stuffing them
Into pigeon holes
And I smelled of sweat and death
And kept drinking until I felt good
Or ran out of money or both
And rode the 14 Mission bus home
With other people like me
Who stared straight ahead or out the window
Or down at their feet

Night shift people like me
Who couldn't do a nine-to-five job
And when I got off the bus
I would huff and puff my way up
Those six long blocks
To my apartment
And pour myself a drink
And turn on the hi-fi
And plop my tired ass down
On the bed
And let Billie Holiday sing
Me to sleep

SOUTH OF MARKET BLUES

High again out where
I don't belong
South of Market Street
Two guys eye each other
In a one-way alley
As six bikers come out
Of a dimly lit bar
Starting up their bikes
Leaving behind crushed beer cans
And rubber skid marks
While further up the street
A pack of jeering teenagers
Taunt an old man
Who wants nothing more than
To survive another night

I walk by trying to look brave
Saying nothing and fearing everything
Ignoring their cat calls
Making it back across town
To the safety of my apartment
Lying naked on the sheets
Sweating nightmares
Real and imagined
Women in black leather
And hi-heel stilettos
That walk up and down
My spine

AQUATIC PARK POEM

In the park
A dog on a leash
Held back by his master
Barking human commands
The dog sits pants
Wags his tail
Dreams a dog's dream
A fire hydrant
A buried bone
Snoopy defeating the Red Baron
Over the skies of Paris

The old man sits down
On the park bench
Daydreams of young women
And Adonis days
A man and his dog
Licking their wounds

LOOKING BACK

When I was young
And down and out
And wrote of pain and agony
From first hand experience
From a small studio apartment
On the fringe of lost souls
Hooker's dopers and low life
I was told by people of affluence
Who liked to hang out with writers
That this was good for me
That great writing came from this
And that some day I would look back
On these days with fondness

At the age of sixty
I moved up to a one-room apartment
In a hip neighborhood
With photographs of Josephine Baker
Billie Holiday Martin Luther King, Junior
And the Kennedy brothers adorning my walls
To remind me of my life long commitment
To civil rights

I managed to stash away
A few bucks in the bank
And my refrigerator and closets
Were nearly full
And at one point in time
I was knocking on the door of success
A door that never quite fully opened

Now when I think back on those days
It's not with any sense of fondness
Though I can't deny that
The women the drugs and the parties
Weren't fun

And the words flowed off the typewriter
In magical splendor
But the people of affluence drifted off too
The apartment the lack of money
The roaches and the mice
Was more circumstance than necessity
And they didn't bring creativity
You can go forward
Or you can go backward
But the smell of shit
Is still the smell of shit
Art creates itself
And I don't think
I'll ever look back on those days
With fondness anymore than
A stockbroker welcoming
The 1929 stock market crash

A MATTER OF TRUST

I no longer trust
These North Beach poets
Re-living the lost generation
Re-living the Beat generation
Their days lost in archives
Their nights wrapped in media hype
The worn pages of their lives
Falling away like costumes
From a cheap clothes rack
Nights meant for writing poems
They spend undressing the dead
Spreading their wasted seed
Like a trail of breadcrumbs
No bird would stoop to eat

GIRLS OF THE TENDERLOIN

The girls of the Tenderloin
Wear tank tops and short tight skirts
With white shoes showing off black skin
Or black shoes contrasting white skin
The girls of the Tenderloin
Strut their stuff from midnight to three
In the morning
Sometimes later if traffic allows

The girls of the Tenderloin
Stand out like a dragon
In A Chinese New Year parade
Moving their hips like
The Hoola-hoops of yesterday
Talking heavy thick slang
Their "hey baby"
You want a date" cutting
Through the air
Like a machete
Looking for a snake
In knee high grass

The girls of the Tenderloin
Walk talk strut their stuff
Not afraid of the law
Man's bluff

The girls of the Tenderloin
Stop traffic with their looks
Their dark brown eyes thirsty
As a Mexican matador looking
For a kill

BURNING OLD POEMS

Going over stacks of poems
from the past
I toss this one and that one
into the fire
Standing back and watching
the flames devour them
Hungry to bury
the mistakes of my youth
The vodka burning
the nerve ends of my stomach
As the poems turn to ash
Ember red
Like a spent volcano
Spitting out seeds of lava
And for one brief moment
I feel a stab of pain
Feeling like a lone mourner
riding a funeral train

WOMAN ON THE BALCONY

I see her two
three times a week
sitting on the balcony
when weather permits
here in old Italy town
in what is left of North Beach
her robe slightly parted
thumbing through the pages of a book
she may or may not be reading
taking no notice of the people down below

Standing to stretch
she yawns with legs sturdy as pillars
that stretch to reach the sky
into the boundaries of my mind
my eyes beg to read the pages
she turns with sensual fingers
wanting just one quick look
one intimate journey into the pages
into the space between
the parting of her robe
a journey into forbidden places
a flight back in time
to another place another world
high on a balcony where I too
ignore the people coming and going
down below

NEW YEARS EVE POEM 2010

Another year passing by
like cloud banks on the horizon
your affair with time doomed
like a failed love affair

Your passion ignited early
burned out like a candle
at the end of its wick

You came in dressed in
a sequin gown and scarf
a coy like promise of a heated
love affair
now you scurry away
like a thief in flight
taking with you
your eleven sisters and brothers
while down at Pier 39
the sea lions bellow their contempt
but you as always shrug your shoulders
and ignore their plaintive call

you with your cold stare
and ice cold breath
that creeps up my spine
makes its way into my blood
soon to head out the door
and rush headlong into the future

how nice it must be to be immortal
born anew year after year
like specs of dust gathering
in the womb of the universe
while I approach my 75th year
doing a slow shuffle down the street
trying to stay one step ahead
of my shadow

JIM'S DONUT SHOP

I sit here on Mission Street
At Jim's Donut Shop
An all night dining delight
Serving scrambled eggs
With green peppers and onions
And just the right amount of grease
2 a.m. bars emptying out
Drunks arriving in assorted states
Of mental undress

I eat slowly listening
To the small talk
Eyeing the speed freaks
And juice freaks

The waitress pushing forty
With folds of fat that hang
From her apron
Like heavy weights
Wears her dress like a teeny-bopper
Leaves behind a trail of thick perfume
That sticks to my skin
Her smile a bloody napkin
Passed on from one tired customer
To another
Like a counterfeit dollar bill
In the hands of a hungry beggar

SITTING AT THE 3300 CLUB

She sits alone
At the 3300 Club
An Irish Bar on Mission Street
Her wrinkled face and baggy clothes
And pulled down hose
Gives the Word "weather beaten"
A new meaning

She sits drinking staring
With no one caring
Her eyes riveted to
The mirror behind the bar
Looking like a pallbearer
Back from a funeral

MISSION STREET BAR

The coin disappears
The jukebox clicks
The record spins
Moves one notch
Drops in the direction
Of the tall brunette dressed
In black leather motorcycle gear

I watch her move in rhythm
As she massages the cue stick
Between her legs
Puts out her cigarette in
The palm of one hand
As if to signal this pussy
Ain't meant to fuck with
As she moves to the back of the room
Like a Saturday night cowboy
Leaves me alone with
A half-finished drink
And a dick in need
Of hard conversation

EASTERN ZEN AND PIG PEN

San Francisco isn't what
She used to be
Not for you and not for me
They have taken the beat
Out of Beat
Forced me to carry
My misery around
Like an underweight Santa Clause
Carrying an empty bag on Christmas day
Life has become nothing more than
Charlie Brown Eastern Zen and
Pig Pen

EATING CHINESE

I like eating Chinese
the tiny hot red peppers
hidden in a spicy sauce
I like lean pork dipped
in hot mustard
I like curried chicken over
a bowl of steaming rice
I like tea and fortune cookies
I like the feel
of chopsticks on my lips
I like Chinese waitresses
in white blouses and bow ties
I like eating Chinese

40th BIRTHDAY POEM

I seem to remember the poet
William Wantling writing a poem
about how he never wanted to be a poet
that he would carry a lunchbox
just like the rest of them
if only the strange mutterings would
leave him alone.

Now at forty
I feel pretty much the same
standing naked as a dead man's shadow
weighed down with these
heavy words locked away inside
these aging brain cells.

Forty years old, feeling like the worn
impression on a buffalo head nickel
holding on to these fading visions
like an immigrant unable
to escape the old country.

the moods coming and going
like cloud banks sinking slowly
like the Titanic
the ghosts dancing on the deck dressed
in words of fire.

And as each day brings yet another illusion
harsh as a hobo's dreams
I sing the song of my chosen grave
the lines dancing like a ballerina
on a high-tension wire.

While a friend of mine considered
a success in the business world
tells me that like him

I should make a list of priorities
and stick by them no matter what
but the hooks are too far in
too high up into the gut
to do anything about.

A poet is like a train
a romantic trip back in time
he is good for a laugh or two
someone to converse with
occasionally sleep with
and always someone
to stay away from when
he is down and out.

America is no place
for a poet to grow old in
a poet is not a thing
I would want my child to be

POEM FOR THE POET WAITING ON FAME

Don't get up in the morning
Pissed-off bent out of shape
Defeated and fatigued
Don't kick your dog
A can is all right
Don't look for trouble
A fist in the face
Won't change history
Don't spit into the wind
It might come back at you
Never place your hand over
Your heart
The marksman might think
You're marking his target
Don't fight the poem
The typewriter is always right
Accept the inevitable
And maybe it won't come until
Next week next month next year
Maybe never
Remember there isn't anything wrong
With being a carpenter
A cab driver a pimp
A whore
Be glad you have two hands
Two feet two eyes two ears
One of the latter is okay
If your last name is Van Gogh
Go easy go slow
Or life will pass you by
Like an aging conductor
Without a train
Leaving you feeling
Like a comic without applause
Know this above all else
Seven out of ten poets

Are bores
And two of the other three
Literary whores
Support that odd one
He/she needs you
And you need him
More than either of you
Will ever know

WALKING THE MISSION ON A HOT SUNDAY AFTERNOON

He's standing on the corner
Looking tough in a tee shirt
And leather jacket
Eighteen going on thirty

He's paring his fingernails
With a pocket knife
A tattoo of a snake
On the palm of one hand

He looks mean
He looks like
He can take care of business
His/yours

Men pass by avoiding
The look in his eyes
He works their fears
Like a disc jockey
In a groove

He wants to be
The main man
The main attraction
Here in the Mission
On a hot Easter Sunday afternoon

WALKING THE STREETS LIKE A COWBOY
LOOKING FOR A MIRACLE

I'm out walking the streets again
Like a crime scene photographer
Past Saint Paul's Church where
The smell of altar boys permeates the air
The ripped-up street still hot
From the smell of tar

The tongues of harlots call out
Like hungry birds dive-bombing for food
Their flapping wings rushing past the head
Of the elderly priest
Standing on the church stairs
Waving his hands frantically in the air
As if in a heated discussion with God
Extending his hand to a wrinkled
Italian woman talking into
Her rosary beads
Dusting off another miracle
Like an aging cowboy back
From a long trail drive

OPEN YOUR EYES

You can't escape it
Your remote control is wed to it
Local and cable channels feed it to you
Like Meat thrown into a lion's cage

News of wars and pending wars
Reel you in like a fish
You become part of it whether
You want to or not

You don't have to be on the front lines
To feel the wounds, see the blood
Taste the carnage

Your parents and grandparents lived it
And willed it to you

The dog feels it every time
He wags his tail
The cat hides under the bed
But can't escape it

Walt Whitman walked the battlefields
Bandaged the wounds of the fallen
William Carlos Williams saw it
In the faces of fallen warriors

They built a cemetery on the lawn
Of General Lee's mansion
General Grant tried to drink the pain away

It's an incurable disease
The Pope is powerless
The President embraces it
The First Lady dances with it
The vampire Congress feeds off it

It's a cancer that eats away at you
Sucks you down like quicksand

God hides in the closet
Takes down notes
Jesus sleeps on a bed of nails

Admirals and Generals run thru the fields
Harvest the dead
Gangster politicians rattle their sabers
In the midnight oil of democracy

Ballistic missiles point at the stars
The firing squads put on alert
Petrified standing like mannequins
In a death field

The businessman's money tree
Shakes In the wind
A nation in slave chains
Disguised as freedom

Turn on the TV
Open your eyes
It's all there to see

UNDER THE LIGHT OF A FULL MOON

born at home premature under
the light of a full moon
I walked the jungles of Panama
fed off Beat Mania
in the streets of North Beach

Shaman poets sang in my ears
under a bed of stars
young women with short skirts
that clung to firm thighs
damp dark cavern
wet as morning dew
peach fuzz dinner
drew me in devoured me
like quicksand

the sweet fragrance of the past
mates with comrades long dead
as I walk back into my birth
work my way through
the sound of water

the wind propels me
towards my destiny
my boyhood gone
like an old jalopy used-up
rusting in an auto junkyard

I head toward the comfort of the now
nailed to the cross of the past
in the language of the present
with no words to light the fire
as I carry the memories like
a mountain climber with
a heavy backpack

vague memories of my mother
singing me to sleep
and the chill of waking
the tongue of dawn cold as dry ice

the hawk sweeps down for the kill
a dog howls at the moon
a cat yawns in boredom
the universe draws new boundary lines
fragile as a new born

the monkey rides the master's back
the coo-coo bird moves backward
into the clock
fearful police lock and load their guns
black boys moving targets
in the night

voter suppression laws
to keep the voting down
southern barbecues
with rednecks hungry
for black "boy" stew

gone the passion of revolution
sell out satisfaction to
the status-quo

the night hound of death
stumbles into the day
the rich roast the poor
like a pig on a spit

labor unions turned into mannequins
fuel the war machine moneymakers
bleed the blood of our youth
like an undertaker dresses the dead

the Roman Senate proceeds unabated
turn out gladiators like machinery parts
endless parades marching bands
waving flags played out like
a Disney Land production

slaves without chains
government without representation
this nation of criminal politicians

the ghost of Custer rises like
a creature from the lagoon
creeps through the night like
a faceless Santa Claus
with a bag of Indian scalps

Allah competes with the Pope
for the rights to the head of Jesus
beheaded by ISIS barbarians
back from a night of slaughter
as the congregation stumbles
like a drunk into the future
carved out in the hands
of a gypsy fortune teller
as I wait out the night in solitude
shut out the demons of insomnia
like a faulty light switch

the holy of the unholy money exchangers
make and pass new laws
laws that feast on the bones
of the poor and dispossessed

a future where animals
turn into animal crackers
and wingless birds hop frantically
around the dinner table

with carving knives in their breasts
serve themselves up as holiday feast

the angels occupy the cheap seats
at Yankee Stadium
God sends down a bolt of lightning
dismayed at the flawed diamond
he created in his image.

SURVIVAL SONG

This poem is for you
Irwin Altman and for
Ed "Foots" Lipman too
For every poet who ever paced
The cellblocks of San Quentin
Folsom, Attica, and Neil Island
Or gave his life in
The peoples struggle of Chile
Cuba or Nicaragua

This poem is for those who walk
The dream of freedom
With guerilla visions
In their hearts and eyes

This poem is for those
Who gave their lifeblood
To wash the streets free of oppression
For those who rest in heroic
And not so heroic graves
In the struggle for human dignity

Poet of blue denim jacket
Mechanic of whispering trees
Walking the execution yard
Over the sleepy tresses of rain
The imaginary and not so imaginary images
Shattering the skull

I sit here alone in my seventy-fourth year
Thinking of long unwritten poems
Thinking of young boys who have fought
The real war
Of grieving mothers and widows
Thinking of innocent girls with color-book eyes
And Young women in black suspender belts
And knee high leather boots
With revolutionary roots

Thinking of how the words come too late
And never say enough
Knowing that in the Buddha Temple of life
All things must die
Knowing there is no survival
No tarot cards horoscopes or incantations
To bring back the dead

I walk the midnight supermarket of death
Thinking of Lorca and that long dirt road
Thinking of the execution wall
The hangman's noose
Ethnic cleansing ovens and genocide
Hearing the gypsy ballad
That sings to the heavens
Knowing there is a strange code
To this language we are addicted too

As Gene Fowler pointed out to me
Evil spelled backwards is live
Being made into a State automated robot is evil
But dying is not evil
For it is in its whole the disintegration
The Bacterial feeding which in turn is a live process
And so the fight goes on and must go on
Until every street has been cleared of assassins
Until every newborn is encircled in a poem

The spirit lives on the vision remains
Even as we retreat into
The depths of our being
Listening to the blood beat solid
Against the hands
Knowing there are secrets in the bones
That cannot be denied or sold out
To the whims of others

Sleep well my brother
Only the flesh is gone
Your strength lives on in those who dare
To reach out and kiss the sun

MEDIA BLUES

don't need the media
to tell me I'm a poet
don't need Ferlinghetti
to discover me
don't need Harper's
to publish me

da Levy dead in Cleveland
Kaufman's ashes floating inside
the belly of a whale
it's a victory of the heart
these words this poetry

don't need to run a marathon
don't need a government grant
don't need a million dollars
just want some pussy
just want to get high
just want to write these words
until the ink
in the pen runs dry

SIX AM POEM

laying here alone in bed
a gnawing hunger in my belly
soon to walk my aging bones
to the kitchen table
take my morning dose of pills
sad there is no woman
to put them next
to my morning cereal

POEM FOR THE POETS WHO FEAST ON THE FLESH OF THE DEAD

There is this certain
Breed of poet
Who sniffs at death
Like a dog sniffs
At a fire hydrant willing
To drop their pants
for a quick shot at fame

They're the paparazzi
Of the literary world
Hang out at funerals
And mortuaries looking
For a photo opportunity

They'll write about anything
And everything from
Princess Diana
To Mother Teresa

They shuffle through life
Like a shackled chain gang prisoner
Draining life's blood
Looking like an undertaker
Dressing the dead

OLD MEN OF SKID ROW

these old men beat
their heads nightly against
the four walls
forced to listen to death's call
the pain so great that
a fifth of whiskey brings
no relief

men who envy those fortunate
enough to escape
men on the verge of suicide
men who wait with nothing
to look forward too
but an obituary column
so small it fits them
like a charm bracelet

WASTED DAYS WASTED NIGHTS

these bars are all the same
the hours pass by
like a freight train
speeding through Fargo
North Dakota

adolescent boys
with stick-shift mentality
between their legs
de-feminized women hawking
their wares, making that
long walk home

left feeling like a pirate
walking a gangplank
morning arriving like a blind man
rattling an empty tin cup

CHRISTMAS 1996

turn the radio off
down a shot of tequila gold
turn the TV on
no war news
first time this month
neighbors cat pays me a visit
one yawn deserves another

I'll spend the night drinking
and writing
sign an armistice
with my troubled soul
let Santa Clause sucker punch
me one more time

TENDERLOIN CAFETERIA POEM II

Busty TS crowds into
The line betrayed by
His Adam's apple

The old man in front
Looks disgusted
Adjusts his toupee with
Purple veined hands
Squints to see the wall
Menu special of the day

Stares straight into
The unsmiling face
Of the counter woman
Arguing with the pimply
Faced bus boy being eyed
By the ageing homosexual
Stirring his coffee
At a corner table

A Jesus freak enters
Selling the new age God
But there are no takers

A poet sits at an empty table
Writing on napkins
Talking into his coffee cup
A hooker works a crossword puzzle
Waiting for the rain to let up

An old woman works her walker
Out the door
Trying to avoid a punk rocker
On roller skates
Who falls into the arms
Of the night priest
Looking Like a pallbearer
With 200 pounds of dead weight

FOURTH OF JULY POEM

stepped on pissed on
cheated and abused
taken advantage of blue collar man
caught up in the American scam
don't tell me anyone
can be anything they want to be
if they put their minds to it
bullshit crap laid on like butter
on the working class stiff
save your message for
the deaf dumb and blind
it'll never sell in the ghetto
or to the immigrants
you've turned your back on
high-fiving jiving court jester
with an act as old as death
out of step reeking from
bad breath
take your message to the church
tell it to the men on death row
tell it to the starving poor
tell it to the sick and lame
tell it to the rich folks
tell it to the politicians
tell it to the serial killers
tell it to the bankers
tell it to Wall Street
tell it to the union busters
tell it to the man on the gallows
tell it to the cowardly terrorists
tell it to the last man at the Alamo
tell it to the chiseled faces on Mount Rushmore
tell it to Madonna
tell it to the street whore
tell it to the last wino on the bowery
tell it to the butcher
tell it to the unemployed

tell it to the circus clown
tell it to the insane
tell it to the outlaw
tell it to the in-laws
tell it to the panhandler
tell it to the conman
tell it to the displaced factory worker
tell it to the elderly
tell it to the re-po man
tell it to the academics
tell it to the poetry politicians
tell it to the last space alien
hiding out in Roswell
tell it to the militia
tell it to the FBI sharpshooters
at Ruby Ridge
tell it to the arsonists at Waco
tell it to the junkie with dry heaves
tell it to the farm worker
tell it to the dishwasher
tell it to the orderlies
tell it to the flag waver
tell it to the tea party
the Chinese peasants working
the rice fields for a dollar a day
tell it to the garment worker slaving away
in sweat shops in Chinatown
and the Latin Quarter
tell it to the garbage man
tell it to corporate America
raping the American worker
tell it to big business
tell it to the oil barons
tell it to the tobacco merchants
tell it to the children addicted
to tv and video games
tell it to the fur industry
who club live baby seals to death

for the clothing merchants
with blood on their hands
tell it to the molested children
tell it to the battered wives of America
tell it to the pharmacy industry dispensing
billions of dollars of drugs each year
tell it to the millions of people
dying from air pollution
in Mexico and abroad
tell it to the man on his deathbed
not sure why he lived
or what he is dying for
tell it to Jesus Christ
shout it to the stars
line the traitors up against the wall
rewrite the Ten Commandments
and start all over again

POEM FOR THE GOVERNOR OF ARIZONA

They cross the border looking
For a piece of the Promised Land
Entering a county that once belonged
To their ancestors

These conquered souls of Mexico
Who toil in fields of abundance
Harvest fruit and vegetables
With stooped backs
And blistered hands
At pay no white man would consider
In a land built by immigrants
It now calls its enemies

FILLMORE BLUES

Black man shooting pool
Black woman singing the blues
Black man playing the horn
Black woman looking like Lena Horne

Outside the black and white patrol car
With its spinning red light
Shotgun in casing heart racing
Big Daddy waits for his cue
Big Daddy waits for his cue

OUTSIDE A BOARDED DOWN JAZZ CLUB

An old man stands in the doorway
Of an abandoned building
Shoulders stooped
Jesus beard ragged clothes
Hands outstretched
Begging for his supper
A tote of wine
His prayers unanswered
Spittle on his chin
Holes in his shoes
Walt Whitman's
Forgotten child

OCEAN BEACH

Old ghosts stand guard
At deserted Play land
At ocean beach
The fat lady sings no more
The funhouse torn down
Like my old high school
The sand dunes filled with debris

A lone ship in the distance
The waves dashing along the shore
Brings back memories of old
San Francisco drowning
In quicksand fog banks
My eyes a piece of dead driftwood
Floating aimlessly out to sea

POEM FOR AN IMAGINARY DAUGHTER

Daughter that I never had
Tugging at my arm-sleeve
From death's still sleep
Hanging heavy as an anchor
Rooted to the tip of my tongue
Your vision riding high in
The retina of my third eye

I toss restlessly in my sleep
A tugboat captain throwing
You a lifeline towing
You gently through my dreams

UN TITLED

A metaphor mated with
A simile after
An orgy with inner rhyme
On a cold starless night
And that's how the
Language school of poets
Was born

STATE OF AFFAIRS

Academic verse
      Empty hearse
East coast
      Milk toast
West coast
      Holy ghost
Academic masturbation
      Forced elation
Language school
      End run
Safe sex
      Condom

LOST SUMMER OF LOVE

We made love in this house
That long ago Summer of Love
The sun banging its head
Against the window shades
Of the old Victorian structure
Where we jammed on the floor
All day and night
Posters of Janis Joplin
And Jimmy Hendrix on the walls
An empty six-pack
A burned out roach for company
Making music with our bodies
As the nine-to-five crowd prepared
Their death march to work

Passing this house
Three decades later
Janis and Hendrix gone
The months the years piled-up
Like liter
I watch a cat in the alley
It's back raised
Staking out its territory
Staring down a would be intruder
Visions of that lost Summer of Love
Flicker inside my head
Ignite a fire extinguished quicker
Than a blink
Death crawling sideways
Up the banister carrying away
My memories in an empty satchel

SOMETIMES THE WORDS JUST WON'T COME

snuck into your bedroom while
you were sleeping
sat at your dresser making
love to your reflection
in the mirror

moving to the side of the bed
I inhaled your fragrance
my mind playing a love ritual
with the soft folds of your flesh
wanting to press my head
between your breasts
between your legs
lick your thighs
articulate my needs
with words that fail me

THOUGHTS ON THE CALIFORNIA DROUGHT

I sit here feeling like a used car
one part after the other failing me
early morning bacon sizzling on the grill

the drought laughs at the masses
teases them with a light drizzle

picture of an old lover stares down
at me from the mantle
her smile warm as the campfire
I sat around as a child

my room a dust garden
my hamstring pull refuses
to address
the promised golden years
drown in tears

Israel and Palestine engaged
in yet another war
Putin playing death games in Moscow
proof the cave man still lives inside us

railroads and monuments built
by immigrants now treated like criminals
the elderly now a liability
the young puppets in a political game
poets once warriors on skateboards
now prisoners of pride and envy

I take refuge in the soft raindrops
the peace of solitude rides my veins
like a steamship treading calm waters
the garden of my mind is still green
poems wait to be planted
in fertile soil no drought can kill.

IT'S HOW YOU LOOK AT IT

sitting here alone
as I've grown accustomed too
listening to Billie Holiday
pounding the computer keyboard
trying to make a little magic
Jack Daniels racing through my veins
having just returned from a book party
celebrating the life of Bob Kaufman
gone like so many others before him
and so many others lined-up waiting to follow
an army of poets sitting on my bookshelf
T.S. Eliot playing the banker
William Carlos Williams suturing wounds
Ferlinghetti in his sailor suit
Kaufman walking the streets of New York
singing his magic with Charlie Parker
Blake playing cards with God
Lorca playing Russian roulette
Gary Snyder building word bridges
and suddenly I'm not alone anymore
the words falling like hard rain

FOR KELL

Approaching sixty-six
Still out there singing
His songs
Playing the guitar
Trying to stay alive
Trying to survive
Makes some people uncomfortable
People who don't want to think
About the down and out
People who don't understand
The other side of the tracks

Last time I saw him
He was dressed in jeans
Black cowboy hat
An old guitar slung around
His back
In an even older carrying case

Pure country
Pure Hank Williams singing
The blues in all of us
With eyes that cry out to be heard

Now approaching 66
Hard as the highway
Bearing his age
He calls Annie on the phone
Reads a poem about
A bird that died in his hand
Remembers the scattering
Of his daughter's ashes

This old time cowboy caught
In the pit of sorrow
This man of music

This one time old friend
Who plays the nerve ends
With the skilled precision
Of a hill man's fiddle
Still fighting still scrapping
Like the rest of us
For whatever time is left

TENDERLOIN CAFETERIA POEM

I have sat
One too many evenings watching
Old men and women
Eat their last meal
One eye on the dessert
The other on the obituary column

POEM FOR THE POET THE WORKING MAN
AND THE UPPER MOBILE YUPPIE

Some people guard their lives
Like a eunuch guards
His master's harem
Like a stockbroker with a hot tip
Like a banker who knows
That today's dollar will only be worth
One-fourth what it is today
In less time than it takes to die
Better to linger over a cup of coffee
Like a skilled lover
With no need for bragging rights

Remember that every meat packer
And fisherman, every waitress
And construction worker knows more
About life than your average poet

The blind man rattling
An empty tin cup
Makes more noise than
A yuppie gunning his BMW
On the way to the grave

THINKING ABOUT THEN AND NOW

when I worked in Modesto
back in 1964
I'd drive to Stockton
and sit in the park
drinking with the winos
in Salinas it was field workers
in Crow's Landing it was
with unemployed Mexicans
at Latino water holes
in North Beach and the Mission
I hung out with deadbeats and fallen angels
street people fighting cirrhosis of the liver
in the Fillmore I cut my teeth on jazz
let Billie Holiday patch up my bleeding heart
in the Portrero I saw the last of the factory workers
grow thinner like their paychecks fearing for their jobs
in the Tenderloin I drank with whores and prostitutes
who opened their pocketbooks as freely as their legs
on Market Street I witnessed panhandlers
crouched like criminals in open doorways
a short distance from the Jesus freaks
with billboards on their backs
pointing the way to heaven
at the old Southern Pacific railway yard
I saw the last of the brakemen
smoking a cigarette with eyes vacant
as an empty satchel
while on the other side of town
high on top of Nob Hill
society ladies sat in chauffeured limousines
white poodle dogs nestled between
their piano legs
unaware of the dredges of humanity
walking third and Howard Street
drinking cheap port from brown paper bags
starving cold disheveled
as the homeless today
waiting for god or pneumonia
to walk them to the grave

RETURNING HOME FROM PANAMA

They had this bar
At Ocean beach called the Chalet
It used to be a hangout for veterans
Of foreign wars
You know the American Legion boys
Sucking up beer and marching in parades
Most of them wrinkled fat and balding
One so old he claimed
To have been gassed in World War One
You never knew whether to believe him or not
He just sat there talking into his beer
Humming his favorite song
OVER HERE OVER THERE
And using terms like Doughboy and pillbox
And you just somehow knew
He had to have been there
Was still there
Would always be there

I HAVE LOITERED

I have loitered at city parks
watching old men
pick their noses
in the twilight of their insanity
I have observed old women
fumble in broken-down purses
for non-existent dreams
I have watched young children
play in scarred sandboxes
destroying sand castles
like soldiers at war

I have observed growing boys
slide down snake slides
chased by keystone cops
sniffing lethal gas
on death's window ledge

I have watched
listened
observed
only to return home
and close the door

VIETNAM WINTER REFLECTIONS

tuned in the television set
down the hall
and turned on the society ball
ticker-tape parade for moon men
Broadway go-go girls doing the swim
burned children crying in my ear
vice president playing on my fears
facts and figures and more government lies
another commercial another young boy dies
heroism found in Vietnam fields
hospital costs rising according
to blue shield
flowers grow and bloom
funeral horses strangle
on gargoyle plumes
baby crying in the background
head so fucked-up can't make a sound
latest love lays naked in upstairs bed
only one goddamn thing going on
inside her head

POEM FOR PADDY O'SULLIVAN

Paddy O'Sullivan
home again wearing the scars
of the past like an engraved bracelet
passed on from one lover to another
walking the streets of north beach
in search of old visions
now only memories in the nightmare
mirror of madness
swapping tales with obscene priests
hung over in the drunkenness
of eternal failure

Paddy O'Sullivan of Kerouac tales
and Cassady visions
Paddy O'Sullivan walking
Washington Square the bulldozer
death lurking everywhere

Paddy O'Sullivan alone in
San Francisco
city of suicides past and present
waiting for that lady poet
who will forgive you in the morning
for forgetting her name
in the hour of dawn
when our needs are soothed
with the power of the written word
that stirs moves inside us
like a runaway express train stalled
in an aging tunnel
like the haunting breath
of a hound dog closing in
for the kill

Paddy O'Sullivan where have
all the poets gone

walking straightjackets
trapped by time
the sun is not as you see it now
the streets are no more or less intense
the lines on your face are the lines
on my face as we move back into
the body into the inner flesh measured
by the amnesia of yesterday

this town coughs up its dead most rudely
the raw nerves of time
returning to haunt me
oblivious to the thirst lying still
at the edge of the river
the blueprint of our life etched in
the dark shadows of the soul

POEM FOR A FRIEND WHO TOLD ME
I NEED TO STOP DWELLING ON THE PAST

a friend of mine tells me
I need to stop dwelling on the past
he says nostalgia is an anchor that
will weigh me down

angels have traded in their wings
for a ticket to my dreams
the phantom of the opera has
a front row seat in my nightmares

mutilated poems wrap themselves
in my arms
pit tomorrow against yesterday

nomadic thoughts camp inside
my brain cells
master to none servant to many

old flames light torches in my loins
there is no place to flee
no resting stop at the end
of a long journey from here
to nowhere

I spend the afternoon
at my favorite coffee shop with
a newspaper for company
tomorrow those same newspaper lines
will be past history
should I pretend they never existed?

I'm ten months into my seventy-seventh year
winter will soon be here
with her cold claws and heavy rain
forcing her way into the walls of my mind

were she of human flesh
she would crack open my memory vault
find miles of past memories that
flow like Li Po poems down
a river old as time
should I ignore her
tell her to come back next winter
that now isn't the time

I have written one too many
memorial poems for friends
who have passed on
should I shut them out of my mind
focus on tomorrow build
a graveled path that leads to the
Promised Land?

my emotions are trapped in quicksand
no place to run no place to hide
endless chatter come from the 4-walls
where death hides between the cracks

the past is my lover
she clings to my body
like a child to a mother's bosom
she sleeps in my memory cells
like a phantom bank that accepts
only deposits refuses withdrawals

I think of her like I think of San Francisco
the City of my birth
the salt air smell at Ocean Beach
the Marina Greens
North Beach and the Fillmore
all filled with memories

my past is my present
the future a gypsy fortune teller

my existence a slow moving locomotive
on an anonymous journey
known only to the conductor
punching invisible tickets in the
hands of faceless passengers

IT SERVES YOU RIGHT TO SUFFER

visions of the past float
like dead wood through
the riverbank of my head
pink panties and white bra
lying on the floor
next to the foot of the bed
drinking tequila with glasses
dipped in salt
as I slowly move down
your soft underbelly
like a moth undressing
a light bulb
feeling like a blind man
learning Braille

I was there the night
you put your fist through the window
swearing you saw God in your own reflection
yelling mantras no one understood
as the people below the window
looked up and wondered what
the screaming was all about

I was there that night at the bar
when you hit the guy over the head
with a beer bottle
leaving seconds before the cops came
and though I should have
I didn't give them your name

I was there the night at the graveyard
when you visited the grave of the only
man you ever loved
and as always you left a bad taste
in my mouth
like a blow job artist bent over

in a back alley
spitting out the seed
like an altar boy hiding
a wafer under his tongue
hoping the priest can't read his thoughts

I was there the night you sat alone
at San Francisco International Airport
with only twenty-five cents to your name
watching people greet their loved ones
at the arrival gate

I was there the night
they took you away
to Langley Porter psychiatric clinic
where you soared like a bird in flight
never to return to earth as we know it

I was there the day
the crucifix-carrying priest
said the black magic mumbo jumbo words
over your grave
looking like a caterer serving food
at an unattended banquet

I was there the day they buried you
in a shawl of unwritten poems
and I drank a toast to you
long after the others left
remembering that white bra
and red lace panties
the night we lifted boulders
from the chest of Jesus
and hurled them in the face
of God

LIFE ON THE STREETS

It's an all night horror show
Hookers pimps transvestites
On the go
It's a night at the Top Of the Mark
Its bathhouses and porno flicks
Lonely vaginas in search of dicks
It's Keystone Cops and neon lights
It's drag queens in tights
It's the Phantom of the Opera
In a grotesque mask
It's a wino blood donor
It's a young man with a boner
It's CNN reporting the news
It's John Lee Hooker singing the blues
It's space aliens hiding out in Roswell
It's poor folks going through hell
It's pilgrims on the way to the shrine
It's police informers dropping a dime
It's politicians wallowing in slime
It's a miracle
It's a crime
It's a million windshield wipers
It's a billion disposable diapers
It's a beautiful rainbow
It's a 24-hour horror show
It's Hank Williams singing:
STOP THE WORLD
I WANT TO GET OFF.
It's doctors practicing
"The hypocritical oath"
It's sport cars and caviar
It's eating pussy and sucking cock
It's Al Capone doing time on the rock
It's a waiter in a bow tie
It's all one God Damn lie
It's the way things are

It's the nature of the beast
It's a famine
It's a feast
It's babies crying
It's old people dying
It's the death of the Beats
It's life on the streets

NORTH BEACH YUPPIE BAR

Hard to believe Jack Spicer
Richard Brautigan once
Drank here
Looking at two businessmen
Playing liar's dice
Here at Gino and Carlo's' Bar
Faces white as piecrust
Double-breasted suits
Italian imported shirts
The legal mafia
Making their own rules

The one with the twisted smile
Hides behind his dice cup
His co-conspirator silently poking
At the olive in his martini glass
Looking like a hit man waiting
To fulfill a contract

REMEMBERING MY GRANDMOTHER

Oh how I hated that third
street hotel
My grandmother old and wrinkled
sitting in the main lobby
with withered men and women
reclining on worn couches
staring off into space
with eyes like death warrants
The smell of death
The smell of funeral parlors
filling the stale air
My grandmother pale and sickly
Her voice trembling
like an earthquake tremor
Rising to hug me
Wearing her years like rosary beads

Oh how I hated those visits
watching those old people
walk in and out of the hotel
on their way to a Sunday walk
or a meal at a Tenderloin cafeteria
looking like wasted corpses
on a 24-hour pass from the morgue
Living behind closed shades
in single light bulb rooms sealed
like tombs, walking in circles
like a mad conductor at an abandoned
railroad yard
Oh how I hated those visits with death
seeing my own mortality
in my grandmother's eyes

The old hotels are gone now
torn down in the name of progress
but they will always exist

in the back of my mind
my grandmother walking
the corridors of my skull
reaching out to me
with bone cold hands
these transitory images
that won't leave me alone
fading in and out like a bad movie

Worn down depressed
I struggle in the morning
to get out of bed
cursed with insomnia
and an arthritic neck
waking two three times a night
with a full bladder
walking down three flights of stairs
to retrieve the morning newspaper
In and out of doctor offices
taking pills like candy
seeing my grandmother
in the dark gloom of that
third street hotel
death crouched low
like a sprinter waiting
the starter's gun

DINING OUT WHEN I WAS YOUNG

I didn't like it when my father
took me with him for lunch
at Compton's Cafeteria
on Market and Van Ness
in San Francisco
It wasn't the food which was
OK
but the old folks that I feared
The cook was fat and bald
and there was no waitress
The bus boy was old
and not a boy at all
and the people who came there
to eat were retired people
on low incomes
with death warrants for eyes
dabbing at their turkey chins
with crumpled paper napkins
looking like pallbearers back
from a funeral

EARLY MORNING SAN FRANCISCO

I rise
6 am to walk the face of dawn
past coffee houses preparing
early morning java
for zombie trance work force
my mind framing textured words
to be laid down on reams of paper
but is it worth the killing of trees
for words so few will see?
El Greco words begging a canvas
plucked from the harp strings of my heart

Jack Micheline's Irish potato neighborhood
Bob Kafuman's Golden Sardine
swimming around inside my head
like a gold fish flushed down the toilet
down to the Mission district
bars opening their doors for the living dead
old men slumped over barstools
with eyes vacant as cattle being led
to the slaughter house
half-Indian Sarah standing
on the corner of 16th Street
looking for a fix
ignoring the police cruiser
with the last of the cowboy cops
looking for a shoot out at
the OK Corral

Got me the slow walk blues
got me a pair of worn down shoes
Pawnshop a-calling
young couple balling
God's messenger with billboard
strapped to his back
looking for Jesus
and finding nothing but
the Wise Men hanging out at
the corner vacant parking lot
dropping a dime for the undercover cop

one step closer to Nirvana
down in the streets of Havana
small town punk goons
straight out of Looney Tunes
leaning against battered old Buick
looking like old time drive-in movie marquee

walking past closed down burlesque house
flashing back to my childhood
the Lone Ranger and Terry
and the Pirates
eaten by locusts and crazed rats

the smell of spring warms the air
while down in North Beach
the last of the Italians wages war
against the Asian immigrants
in a territorial dispute over who owns
the rights to the bocce ball courts
at Aquatic Park

no more will I be an agent
for the demons camped inside
my head
let them write their own poems

walking these streets is wearing me out
I keep slipping into the past
in a failed attempt to communicate
with the future

my life has become a marathon walk
leading to endless coffee shops
taken over by expressionless aliens
with laptop computers and cell phones
rising each morning like a prisoner
waiting the executioner's gun
the years hung out to dry
like old underwear
on a frail clothesline

MARTHA'S COFFEE SHOP

we live on marked time
the calendar ticking down
like a bomb strapped
to the chest of a suicide bomber
sitting at the park,
the beach, coffee houses
watching young lovers
with no perception of time
eyes like a child watching
a magician for the first time

here at Martha's Coffee Shop
on Church street
I sip on my coffee
hot as the passion I witness
two young lovers holding hands
necking like only the young can neck
unashamed tongues locked as one
his hand on her bare knee
as I measure my life
with the stirring of a spoon
my taste buds wanting forbidden fruit
long out of reach

THE OLD ITALIANS OF AQUATIC PARK

the old men of Aquatic Park
are dying or dead
they spend their time playing
bocce ball
lady death striking them down
like bowling pins
the old men of Aquatic Park
are steeped in tradition
dark skinned dressed in sport
shirts and loose-fitting slacks
looking like bit actors
in a 1950's movie
dancing the Last Waltz
on the deck of the Titanic

the old men of Aquatic Park
sit on hard wooden benches
late in the afternoon
their eyes moving left, right
front, center as if at a tennis match
pausing to feed the pigeons
using their hands like cutting knives
to separate the crust from the bread
which they toss into the air
like rice at an Italian wedding
rising to brush the crumbs
from their baggy trousers
one with a suit vest and tie
pulls at the gold chain
holding his pocket watch
tucked securely next to his heart

the old men of Aquatic Park
have the smell of garlic and pasta
embedded in their skin
Italy beating in their hearts

the old men of Aquatic Park
are dying off with grace and dignity
and a love for the old ways

there is something sad
about being Americanized
there is something sad
about growing old
the bocce ball rolls slowly
along the grass lawn
coming to rest like a hearse
parked next to an open grave

funerals wait on them
flowers scattered like empty promises
the mourners growing fewer in number
their ranks depleted
file slowly into their cars
disappear into the shadows
of late afternoon monotony

bocce ball will resume
in the morning
there are pigeons to be fed
wine to drink
stories to tell
the thirst for life masked
in the face of death

SAN FRANCISCO BLUES

bombings rape ethnic cleansing
Bill Gates Ted Turner and the Pope
all selling their own brand of dope
a mayor who is a joke
a bus system that doesn't work
head cases set loose on the street
punk rockers with rainbow colored hair
women with pierced genitals
Viagra for the disinterested
Ginseng for tired blood

my illusions are fighting a duel with
my delusions
the last time I picked up
a white courtesy telephone
the voice on the other end was mine

the dates on my calendar are blank
the pinball machine has no flippers
there's no prize in my crackerjack box
my radio plays nothing but commercials
my hand holds my cock in contempt
my love life is an unread resume
with one too many references

I dreamt I was a gunrunner
trading hardware for software
I want my photo on a cereal box
not a milk carton

the IRS is a legal shake down
the Pentagon a slaughterhouse
Jack the Ripper sliced and diced
his way though life
and he wasn't even a chef

Freud was impotent
but put on a good show
Monks know the truth
but won't share it
you know you're in trouble
when your shrink deals in fantasies
and leaves you with his reality
my life has become a distraction
no additions and subtractions
when it becomes an abstraction
I'll know I've found success

NO QUESTIONS ASKED

You think you know me because
We share the same bed
Know where I work
What restaurants I frequent
You think you know me because
You've sucked my cock
Made the bed cleaned the house
On a scale of one to ten
I'm off the charts
You think you know me because
I've gone down on you
Pick you up after work
Rub your back
Vote the same political party
You think you know me because
You read my poetry
Cry with me
      Fuck with me
Laugh with me
      Cum with me.

Don't make me laugh
It's all a disguise
Desperate for attention
Desperate for love
Desperate for a meaningful relationship
Dinner by candlelight
Valentines 365 days a year
When life is seldom more than
A series of sitcoms with an occasional
Blockbuster movie thrown in

I don't want Wonder Woman
I don't want a partnership
I don't want a twelve step program which
Is eleven steps too many

I'm not into leather or genital torture
Physical or mental mind games

I don't want to bond
I'm not looking for a tennis match
I don't want my ego massaged
I'm not looking for an alternative
Life style
I don't want a bimbo
I don't want a mannequin
I don't want a homosexual
A lesbian or a bisexual
I don't want a perfect ten
Or a woman who will tell me how
Where and when
I don't want a trip to Rome
I'm not interested in glory holes
Or butt holes
I don't want to meet your mother
Your sister or your brother
Or to make your heart flutter
I don't want a Ford Mustang
Or know about the Big Bang
Or hang around with the gang
I don't want parity
I don't seek your charity
I don't want mathematical equations
Or clandestine meetings at train stations
I don't want to go to midnight mass
Or fuck you in the ass
I don't want you to dress in buttons and bows
Or to lick your toes
I don't want to show you up on the dance floor
Or to make you my private whore

All I want is for me to be me
You to be you
A chance to see another day through
All I want is to take one day at a time
Never have to make a poem rhyme
All I want is to be here in bed
Lying next to you
No questions asked
No faces to unmask

FOR JILL

It was late summer
And Cigar was going after
His tenth straight win
The papers had him pegged
At better than even odds
And five minutes before post time
My woman steps out of the shower
Buck naked smelling
Like a rose bush
And something inside me says
I'm going to have my own
Kentucky Derby
As she straddles me on top
And begins a race of her own
I hear the announcer on TV
Say the horses are at the starting gate
But by then we're heading for
The home stretch

Seconds before we cross
The finish line
Cigar is in the winner's circle
But I can tell from the look
On my lover's face
That the real winner never left
The starting gate

LET'S GET REAL

There is this small press magazine
A real fine magazine with
A real fine editor
Except for a fixation for living legends

In a recent issue of the magazine
The chosen legend was described
As wanting nothing more than happiness
Passion, justice, sex and the means
To take care of his family
Much like the old Republican contract
With America

It made me ask myself
Isn't this what we all want?
Well maybe not all of us
I mean I know some friends of mine
Who would settle for sex and booze

This legend poet was described
As writing incessantly and consistently
And getting his work out to read which
May or may not be a virtue
Given the current state of small
Press literature

The only legend I came across
Who fit this description
Was Charles Bukowski although Lyn Lifshin
Certainly gets her work out to be read

The more I read the more puzzled
I became
I mean was this poet
A real legend
Did he rob banks like Jessie James

Do his exploits rival those of Bonnie
And Clyde?
Perhaps he was one of the original
Nashville C&W outlaw singers?

I kept asking myself over and over
What makes a legend?
I mean there aren't many outlaw poets
Out there today
And if they carry guns
They shoot blanks
And none have a bounty on their head
The law having laid them to rest
Back in the sixties and seventies

Don't get me wrong
I'm not knocking this legend's work
I've read his poems here and there
And they are decent enough
And deserving of publication
It's the title they have hung around
His neck that bothers me
Much like the noose around a horse thief
In the good old days when
Legends were born

I mean let's be honest
How many under forty year old
Living legends do you know?
Janis Joplin, Hank Williams
Jimmy Hendrix, Buddy Holly
But they were musicians
And had to die for the title

The only true legend I knew
Was the poet Bob Kaufman
But outside of North Beach and France
How many people have read his work?

Having once edited a literary magazine
For seventeen years
I have watched the new poets
Replace the old poets
And that's the way it should be
But I hung around with a lot
Of damn fine poets
Some of them still living
But I can't recall any of us
Seeing ourselves as legends
Though maybe a bartender or woman or two
Might have seen us in this light
But not for anything we wrote

In this tribute to the living legend
We are told he is basically honest
Basically the word I question
Though none of us are 100% honest
Not even with ourselves
Not me, not you, not the editor
Of one of the finest
Literary magazines around

Honesty is a word to often abused
Integrity is a better word
For if you still have your integrity
When you're lying there on your deathbed
If you can look death in the eye
And spit in her face and say
FUCK YOU
And you know in your heart
That in your next lifetime
You won't be called on to work off
A hundred years of bad karma
Then maybe just maybe
You'll have earned the right
To be called a legend

ONE TOO MANY POETS

you can find them
in the back room
poised for a quick exit
they're the first poets
to read and the first
to leave

they always carry their work
with them in loose-leaf notebooks
they always have a pretty woman
hanging on to their arm
there is always one
who claims to have known
Kerouac or Ginsberg
another one who claims
to have slept with one or both

they're usually sandwiched
in between a headache
or a hangover or two
2 or 3 live with the gods
another 2 or 3 claim
they are God

there is usually one
who claims to have
Indian blood
and who is there
looking to get laid

2 ex-junkies
1 homosexual
a drag queen
with too much mascara
2 sad-eyed women rubbing
their hands when they would

prefer to be rubbing something else

always a dropout
from the beat generation
a holdover from
the hippie days
a woman with short hair
a nervous poet with a tic
a refugee from the drug set
a failed poet
who drops names faster
than an auctioneer

one poet who reviews poetry
one poet who's an editor
one poet who was an editor
one poet who wants to be an editor
one messiah and one visiting
out of town star

POEM FOR MY FIRST LOVE

Seven months into
my 77th birthday
I slip back in time
I'm driving down
Highway One where
California fertile hills wink at me

giant trees and seashore merge as one
cloudbanks ride the horizon
like Chief Red Cloud rode the plains
in search of the last buffalo

sweet mangos and watermelon wine
sweet as cotton candy stuck
to the roots of my tongue
fed my youth nourished my spirit
the poem the language of my soul
your body indented against mine
hot as an iron pressed to a garment

a youthful hunger that knew no bounds
feasted like a condemned man devouring
his last meal
the way Eskimos used to swallow
the tears of the dying
to keep the one gone
with them

FROM MY WINDOW

I watch him shadow boxing
In his living room
His curtain open
Free admission
No questions asked
A giant Doberman
Ears perched back
In attack mode
Watching panting
As the old man weaves
Ducks Shadow boxes
An imaginary opponent

From my vantage point
Across the way
I watch him jab
A left hook an upper cut
And was that a Kid Gavilan
Bolo punch?
Duck bob and weave
No trainer no corner man
To throw in the towel

I imagine him in the ring
Bleeding out of breath
Knocked down
Taking the mandatory
Eight count
Getting back up again
Beating the ten count
Knowing that like
The rest of us
He can't win
Can't beat the odds
But refusing to throw
In the towel

Nose bleeding
Head pounding
Jabbing punching
Going the distance
Hoping to get something
Better than a draw

INSOMNIA

Tossing turning
Praying for sleep
When all else fails me
But God has no time
For insomniacs
And Christ must be busy
Preparing for the resurrection
Falling asleep for an hour or two
Head churning buttermilk dreams
The Holy Ghost stops by for a chat
Seems like an amicable chap
Swaps stories from the past
Just as if he were one of the boys
As I gradually surrender to his will
Dreams lined-up like shots of tequila
At a Mexican brothel
Only to wake again and again
Insomnia a heavily armored
Spanish conquistador
Takes no prisoners
Plays your mind like a card shark
Your body like a whore
In the morning leaves you feeling
Like bits and pieces of a shipwreck
Washed up along the shore

66

Lines beginning to form
At the corner of my eyes
And I eat not from hunger
But from force of habit
The fire in the loins
Is still there
And the hose still hard
But no one to man it

SEVENTY

The words come harder
Set their own pace
Sometimes the turtle
Sometimes the hare
But always stripped bare
Bukowski told me in a letter
You seem like a man
Who knows where it's at
Didn't then don't now
Just hanging around
With words that dangle
Like an outlaw's neck stretched
At the end of a rope

SEVENTY-ONE

I like wild women
Who drink straight shots
I like demure women
Who look like librarians
And wear long dresses
That touch the floor
But I've retired from the game
Although not of my own choosing
Forced to sit on the sidelines
And eyeball the show
Watching young women walk by
With pert breasts and jiggling butts
My cock rising to half-mast
A false promise lost in skipped heartbeats
That plays tricks with my shadow
Trailing behind me
Like an old junkyard dog
Walking behind his master
Hoping for table scraps

WINTER POEM

It's been in the thirties
Two nights in a row
And I'm sitting here freezing
My ass off with a hacking cough
Waiting for the power company
To come and fix the problem
But it isn't so bad
When you consider 9/11
The war on Iraq
The earthquakes in Haiti and Chili
And that d.a. levy took a rifle
Between his legs
And blew his brains out
Which has nothing and yet everything
To do with this poem

Thirty-degree nights won't kill you
But they don't bring comfort either
The trouble with being single
The trouble with being seventy
Is knowing you could die alone
And go unnoticed for weeks
With nothing but rotting flesh
To tell your story
And a few poems to remember
You by

DINING OUT WHEN I WAS YOUNG

I didn't like it when my father
took me with him for lunch
at Compton's cafeteria
On Market and Van Ness
in the heart of San Francisco

It wasn't the food
that was OK
but the old folks I feared
the cook was fat and bald
and there was no waitress
the bus boy was old
and not a boy at all
and the people who came there to eat
were retired people on low incomes
with death warrants for eyes
dabbing at their turkey-chins
with crumpled paper napkins
looking like pallbearers
back from a funeral

RANDOM WORD POEM

Snow light warm dream
    Blue morning woman
Sweet spring sparks love
    Like humming bird
In Green garden mind

BACK FROM AN MRI

Back from an MRI brain scan
I listen to a Miles Davis album
Black Hawk San Francisco 1962
where a young Latina and I grooved
on the vibes

Here at home
jazz in my head jazz in my bed
jazz waking up the dead

Miles, Charlie Parker, and Lester Young
serenade an army of poets sitting
on my bookshelf:
T.S. Eliot playing the banker
Walt Whitman walking the battlefields
Williams Carlos Williams suturing wounds
Kaufman walking the streets of New York
Juggling a "Golden Sardine"
Blake playing cards with God
Lorca playing Russian Roulette
Micheline dancing with Mingus
Gary Snyder building word bridges
and suddenly I'm not alone anymore
the words falling like soft rain
in a winter green garden

MONDAY MORNING POEM

Smell of spring in the air
Misty fog gives way to light rain
Cars spewing deadly exhaust fumes
Windshield wipers flapping like the
Wings of birds in migration
Stone faces hidden behind steering wheels
Give no quarter except for the
Red stoplight as pedestrians
Looking like mannequins
Scurry across the street
On the way to work
Boarding the morning bus
Pressed together like preserved butterflies
Between the pages of an antique book

THE WORLDS LAST RODEO

Strange this trip back in time
Not with flesh and blood
But in disguise of poems
Having survived all these decades
The muscles the cells changing dying
And yet somehow managing to survive
Traveling through a time tunnel
Through an origin you cannot remember
Because there is no you to remember it
Walking behind my shadow
Shedding the years like a snake sheds its skin

I who have never called myself a poet
Never clothed myself in consonants and vowels
Nor took refuge in metaphors
Yet planting the words on the page
Like a florist preparing a bridal banquet
A tender arrangement of flesh and bones
At war with the demons camped inside me
Who leave behind a Custer massacre of words
Left cooking these images
Like a fry cook scrambled over easy

Waking at three in the morning
With junkie like sweats
My eyes a heat seeking missile
Honing in on an invisible kill
Left feeling like an alcoholic with DTs
Trying to roll a cigarette
Atop a bucking bull
At the world's last rodeo

POEM FOR A FRIEND IN PRISON

Hello Joe
I could handle the name change
but they keep transferring you
to so many different units
I'm running out of space
in my address book
and now they're shuffling you
from prison to prison

I know this is America
but this is a bit too much
even for a pro like me
all these prisons being built
like factory assembly lines
I mean there's only so many
license plates one can make
makes no sense to me

You ask how I'm doing which
is kind of you
given your circumstances
truth is I'm confined to my own prison
even if there are no keepers
where life has become a surreal movie
with nothing but bit actors
like those old time sing-a-longs
they flashed on the screen
when I was a kid
follow the bouncing ball
trouble is I couldn't then and can't now
carry a tune

It's a hard life brother
on the inside on the outside
The old man down on Market Street
the one with no legs and a skateboard

has more balls than Congress
this is a bitch of a poem
not a bitching one
I know you know the difference
even if your jailers don't
thirsting after blood
like a junkie lab technician stepping
on over and around dead bodies
looking for new spirits to bury

The message of America can't be found
on Mount Rushmore
it's written in blood
at the Texas Book Depository

I know this guy who believes
if we reduce the world population
by a third and close our borders
there will be enough food for everyone
in the world
but this same guy breeds killer dogs
and has five children
and another on the way
it's the kind of shit that's driving me sane
just when I was getting the insane part
down to perfection

Better watch it brother
you might get what you wish for
a new trial a new judge a new jury
but would the outcome be any different?

The D.A. could wear a black robe a wig
powder his cheeks
bend over and beg forgiveness
what's left of Eliot Ness' old gang
could take on the Wise Guys outside
the courthouse

hell I might even buy a ticket
and mouth a few obscenities
to take the edge off the hype

We are born we die
we spend time in between
be it behind or outside the walls
and the prisons keep getting built
and all I can do about it
is write these "bitching" poems
to an audience that does nothing but bitch

Sometimes I think
I'm a retarded space alien
put here by a superior race
you on the inside me on the outside
inner parts of a human computer waiting
to be blanked from the screen

HOW I WANT TO BE REMEMBERED

Play me some Willie Nelson
And Johnny Cash
Toast me with some sour mash
Have six young girls do a dance
One hooker in leather vest and pants
Carry my ashes to the top of Mount Davidson
With a lone Monk trailing behind

Chocolate truffles and champagne served at sunset
No open bar, free to all.
Irish Whiskey vodka and tequila
Served by a French lass with a saucy ass

Set up speakers on each side of the hill
Play some poetry by Kaufman and Micheline
Blast some Dylan to the birds overhead
Stir the juices in the living dead

Put a shot glass in the box carrying my ashes
A pen and a sheet of blank paper.

No flowers No tears
Just that Lone Monk doing
A Buddhist chant

Let the sunset be my headstone
My poems my marker

HOSPITAL POEM

so many hospitals with
so many names of so many people
it makes the heart want to bleed
Saint Francis Saint Mary's
Saint Joseph Saint Luke's
Saint this one and that one
so many people lined-up waiting to die
hacking coughing spitting up their insides
so many nurses with dollar bill eyes
strutting their stuff into the parking lot
too tired for love
too tired to laugh
overcome with failure and fatigue
so many doctors
so sad they can't be God
hiding their disappointment
in cocktail glasses or between
the legs of the angels of mercy
so many cardiac arrests
so many dead on arrivals
so many John Doe's
so many Jane Doe's
how many only
the business office knows
and the security guards
and the house keeping staff
and the accountants
and the gray haired lady volunteers
with eyes worn as an Indian head penny
and the young nurses with bodies
sweet as orange blossoms
who walk it on by your door
and my door
worn down stepped on
they eat and sleep
and masturbate

with hands and vibrators
some none to cleverly
some like Van Gogh
returning each day
to walk the halls like vampires
with painted fingernails
that slices the flesh to the bone

the doctors the nurses
the orderlies in white
the priests the patients
and the loved ones
all seeking a private audience with God
here behind these sterile walls where
death stalks the halls with panting breath
licking the crevice of the soul
death the noble savage
death the avenging sadist leaving behind
her scars
playing out the game to the bitter end
a giant hearse among
a sea of compact cars

NEW YEARS DAY POEM

some things stick in your mind
like dental cement
like your first kiss
the JFK assassination
the wild years, a trip down
highway 101
foot stuck to floor pedal
hugging the middle lane
at one hundred miles an hour
a wild tango that turns into a shuffle

I like five in the morning walks
alone with my thoughts when
the shops are closed
and people still asleep
my neighborhood a ghost town
still as a lion waiting on its prey
the silence a monk in meditation
with no need for explanation

2010 gone...
the revelry put to rest
insomnia driven
I greet 2011 alone
with words that bleed
for company

A poem forms nibbles
at my brain cells
a beggar hungry for food
but the cupboard is empty
as I retreat into the amnesia
of yester-year
the lost treasure of my youth
a pirate with a graying beard
boarding a ghost ship rocking
aimlessly at sea

POEM FOR JACK MICHELINE

Hey, Jack
The Poetry Flash finally
Gave you some space
Even if you had to die for it
They used your name in
The same sentence as Genius
Funny when you were alive
You never heard that
The Iowa Review
The Paris Review
The American poetry Review
And their minions

This is not poetry
Whatever happened
To Walt Whitman's wild children?

The holy grail has gone
The way of grand slams
Con games and cheap scams
These people dance with the dead
They have never drunk
A cup of thick black coffee
At an all night truck stop diner
Or walked with holes in their shoes
Or sang the blues

They shop at Malls
Browse the web
For their names
They don't make love
They fuck
They don't eat food
They nibble
They don't drink
They sip

It's becoming nothing more
Than an ego trip
You won't find them
In the Mission
In the Tenderloin
Or South of Market Street
Or standing in the $2 line
At the race track

They drink bottled water
Eat sushi
Trade favors like baseball cards
They're living proof
Of mediocrity in the arts

They're the gravediggers
Of the beats
Playing trick-or-treat
They never miss getting quoted
In an obituary
They're the paparazzi
Of the poetry world
Always looking for
A photo opportunity
They don't know the meaning of shame
To them poetry is a monopoly game

Hungry for money
Hungry for power
Hungry for fame
These would-be mountain men
Who set their traps with
The skills of a gravedigger

This is the new breed poetry politician
Seasoned alley cats
Hiding in sand boxes
Sharpening their claws

Looking for the right back to scratch
Staking out their territory
Like a vampire
In need of a fresh fix of blood

Their faces are puffy
Their handshakes weak
They hover in the shadows
Like an undertaker waiting
To dress the dead

Beware my friends
Don't die
They'll be sniffing
At your grave

GHOSTS FROM THE PAST

I drove the freeway to Tucson
1960's Hippie Era
pulled over twice by the police
long hair and California license plates
got me two citation warnings
three days in redneck country
was like a year drinking at Western bars
with cowboys who eyed me like
I was an Indian escaped from
the reservation
unsure why I had come here
nothing beautiful nothing natural
except for the stunning evening sunset

a poet friend calls me says
Ginsberg has flown back from India
to become the resident guru
of the Haight Ashbury
as I rack up another warning ticket

cowboy drunks give new definition
to the word redneck
no room for compassion here
no room for poets
words like a campfire
with no match to light them
die in the desert heat

I pull up roots drive north
the death mask sunset
rides a passing cloud

I stop in the desert
pop open a bottle of water
have a one way conversation
with a cactus plant

wonder what my shrink
would think
the beauty of solitude
I could have a million conversations
in a single morning dialogue

I return home keep
a notebook by my bed
write down my dreams
but when I wake in the morning
someone else's handwriting
is on the pages

No one will identify
the blood between the lines
see the ghosts walk the halls
restless souls from my past
like a starving wolf
in the dead of winter
looking to fill his hunger
on wild game
or words that cling to flesh
like a leech to an open wound

WASTE LAND OF BLURRED VISIONS

I know this poet who plays
The Poetry Biz game
Knows how to trade favors
In 24 different flavors
His days pass faster than the
Muteness of his message
Seriousness is being treated like a sickness
A cancer to be avoided
Its grand slams and elite poetry festivals
Run by Grand Marshals and their elves
The wasteland of blurred visions
Lies like an idle landmine waiting
To explode in the minds of circus clowns

My poet friend has money in the stock market
Money in the bank
Money under his mattress
He's like a stand-up comedian
A burlesque dancer with see-through fans
To him a crisis is a loose bowel movement
A skipped heartbeat or two
But what of the crisis of the social system
A system of calculated murder
A system of chemical and environmental cancer
A system of the poor and elderly
A system of sadness
How do I laugh about this
How do I laugh about my brothers in prison
My dead comrades racing across blood stained clouds
Their bruised feet bringing down rain
A rain that does not cleanse but
Leaves behind scars and torn flesh
And still the games go on
Red poets who write love songs for Stalin
Populist poets turned businessmen
Hanging out at coffee houses
And uptown bars

Hoping for a lottery chance at fame
I can't wear the easy grin
It is an ill-fitting suit
My mind is a tailor who fits
Me with needled threads
And yes there is a place for laughter
And I too can pen a funny line
But poetry is more than laughter
More than stepping up on stage
One hand on the poem
The other on the applause meter
And it was a Russian poet who said
"The function of poetry must be
To make us blush with shame."
And it was an American poet who said
"The dams reverse themselves and want
To go stand alone in the desert"
That is why these poems are sad
The long-dead running over the fields
The masses sinking down
The light in the children's faces
Fading at six and seven
These are the voices I heed
Knowing the poet must believe
In what he says and writes
That a poet's responsibility
Goes beyond the written word
A poet must be angry
But he must be able to sing too
His words must melt like sweet honey
On a blistered tongue
For flat-backed whales sing and birds sing
But my poet friend has forgotten how to sing
It shows in his eyes
It shows in his nervous laughter

My poet friend writes 365 poems a year
He spends his time in coffee houses courting
The favors of those in power

He does not visit the jails
The prisons the forests the urban slums
The freezing North Dakota dawn
He does not feel the whisper
Of the secret that passes over the plains

CALL TO POETS

Poets unite
forget about a career in poetry
and concentrate on the poem
quit turning out factory
assembly line poems
quit trying to imitate Bukowski

Poets unite
listen to your brothers and sisters
quit being the first poet to read
and the first one to leave

quit using words as a preaching tool
when all over the world people are dying
victims of murder and genocide
as we stand on stage
well fed begging for applause
playing to the audience
telling our most intimate secrets
pretending to be knowledgeable
when we know so little

rams out fucking sheep
poets playing trick-or-treat
politicians beating their meat
whores making it under the sheets
predators lined up with elbow grease
landlords waiting to cancel your lease
it's gotten so bad that you can't tell
the real from the elite
everyone wants to become a carbon copy
of themselves

Take a number step up on stage
rattle the cage
let loose your rage

be sure to have your
cell phone on
(the call you miss may be
from god)
as we rival Ringling Brothers
standing tall standing proud
working the crowd

I call for all poets
to put down their pens
for a year
take a vow of silence
serve a holiday meal
at Saint Anthony's
quit sending out manuscripts
for six months a year
spend the saved postage
helping the homeless
sell your signed copies
of Bukowski and Ginsberg and
give the proceeds to war victims
in Iraq and Syria

pay homage at Malcolm X's grave
ride a boxcar for Woody Guthrie
say 12 Hail Mary's for Ali
sing a song for Selena
say a prayer for Allen
take the Eskimo out of Eskimo Pie
rename Hooters bar "testicles"
and hire male waiters to serve
in jockey shorts

legalize prostitution
campaign to have cops arrested
for disturbing the "peace"
tell the pope that you're giving up
drugs and the church to worship
at the altar of Walt Whitman

make Patchen required reading
adopt a rescue dog
volunteer for Meals on Wheels
deliver food to the disabled and dying

give up center stage ego driven mania
for a trip to the park at dusk
invest in yourself instead of interest
bearing bank accounts

meditate instead of masturbate
make love instead of fucking
drop a bomb on Naropa
to prove you're more than
a poet junkie

take a bookstore owner to dinner
talk child talk translate gibberish
put ego aside put power aside
quit visiting Kerouac's and
Bukowski's graves

return to the real world
put the poet back in poetry
make me want to believe
in you again

WINTER POEM II

rain-drops seek refuge
on my windowsill
ghosts from my past make love
to my brain cells like
a moth drawn to a light bulb
crawl up my spine
take root in my heart
explore my bones like
an undertaker dressing the dead
mock the birds strung out like
bowling pins moments before flight

rolling thunder awakens my senses
sends shivers through the pores of my skin
march like fire-ants up and down my spine
my body an ancient tree bends with time
poems tossed aside like
leftovers from a holiday feast
I an aging shaman
a shadow within a shadow
an old Model "T" Ford
cranked-up for one last ride

dead comrades serenade me
the sweet smell of orchids takes
residence inside my nostrils
ladies of the night fan my fevered brow
unwritten poems pass through my eyeballs
seek refuge in the attic of my mind
sand storms devour my thoughts
bind to me like glue

demons spit at me
hot as an over-heated radiator
faceless ancestors pile up like
bones in an elephant graveyard

an armada of Viking funeral ships
buck the currents of the sea
left alone in a frenzy of raindrops
an aging tightrope walker without
a safety net

TRUMP LAND

I cannot pledge allegiance to a racist
Who stands behind the flag
Whose principles you defile

I will not bow down to Corporate America
And its religious right

I cannot accept your moral bankruptcy
Your greenback God selling lives
On the stock market exchange

I will not bow down to a country where
Immigrants are treated like criminals
And women as chattel

A country whose papal church
Has its own bank where
Ka-ching ka-ching is the new holy mantra

America you have become
One big insane asylum
Your manic depressive innkeepers
Waging war on the masses

Your henchmen standing proud
On your purple majestic mountains
Kissing the cold stone faces on Mount Rushmore
Where you measure your inclusion
Looking like a Mafia Don with the
Cold kiss of death on your breath

INDEX OF TITLES
AND FIRST LINES

Poem titles are in bold italics and the first lines are in regular text with page numbers on the right.

a friend of mine tells me 125
A Matter of Trust 70
A metaphor mated with 109
Academic verse 110
After my shift at Rincon Annex 65
air has that stale cigarette smell, The 47
An old man stands in the doorway 106
Another year passing by 2010 74
Approaching sixty-six 115
Aquatic Park Poem 67

Back From an MRI 161
Back from an MRI brain scan 161
Black Hawk 1963, The 54
Black man shooting pool 105
bombings rape ethnic cleansing 141
born at home premature under 88
Burning Old Poems 72
Busty TS crowds into 100

Call to Poets 179
Chinatown Sweat Shop 51
Christmas 1996 99
City Happenings 64
City Poet 43
Cocaine Annie 49
cocaine Annie biker queen 49
cop's flashlight intruding on my thoughts 45

d.a. Levy was dead right	52
d.a.Levy Was Dead Right	52
Daughter that I never had	108
Dining Out When I Was Young	135
Dining Out When I Was Young	159
don't need the media	94
Early Morning San Francisco	136
Eastern Zen and Pig Pen	78
Eating Chinese	79
Fillmore Blues	105
For Jack Micheline	59
For Jamie	53
For Jill	145
For Kell	115
Fourth of July Poem	101
From My Window	152
Ghosts from the Past	174
Girls of the Tenderloin	71
Going Back in Time	44
Going over stacks of poems	72
Hard to believe Jack Spicer	132
He sleeps in doorways	59
He walks the streets of North Beach	57
He's standing on the corner	84
Hello Joe	164
Hey, Jack	171
High again out where	66
Hospital Poem	168
how I used to get into	48
How I Want to be Remembered	167
I am San Francisco	39
I cannot pledge allegiance to a racist	184
I didn't like it when my father	135

I didn't like it when my father 159
I drove the freeway to Tucson 174
I Have Loitered *121*
I have loitered at city parks 121
I have sat 117
I have witnessed the waterfront decay 39
I know this poet who plays 176
I like eating Chinese 79
I like wild women 157
I no longer trust 70
I rise 136
I see her two 73
I seem to remember the poet 80
I seem to remember the poet 82
I sit here feeling like a used car 113
I sit here on Mission Street 75
I was looking at my scrapbook the other night 44
I watch him shadow boxing 152
I'm out walking the streets again 84
I've walked these San Francisco streets 61
In the park 67
Insomnia *154*
It Serves You Right to Suffer *128*
It was late summer 145
It's an all night horror show 130
It's been in the thirties 158
It's How You Look At It *114*

Jazz Angel *55*
Jim's Donut Shop *75*

laying here alone in bed 95
Let's Get Real *146*
Life on the Streets *130*
Lines beginning to form 155
Looking Back *68*
Lost Summer of Love *111*

Martha's Coffee Shop 138
Media Blues 94
Memories 56
Mission Street Bar 77
Monday Morning Poem 162

New Years Day Poem 170
New Years Eve Poem 2010 74
No more jazz at the Black Hawk 56
No need to go out to a movie 46
No Questions Asked 143
North Beach Yuppie Bar 132

Ocean Beach 107
Oh how I hated that third 133
Old ghosts stand guard 107
Old Italians of Aquatic Park, The 139
Old Joe 58
Old Men of Skid Row 97
Old Warrior of North Beach 57
Once addiction sets in 43
One Too Many Poets 149
Open Your Eyes 86
Outside a Boarded Down Jazz Club 106

Paddy O'Sullivan 123
Play me some Willie Nelson 167
Poem For a Friend in Prison 164
Poem for a Friend Who Told Me
      I Need to Stop Dwelling on the Past 125
Poem for Alexsey Dayen 60
Poem for An Imaginary Daughter 108
Poem for Jack Micheline 171
Poem for my First Love 151
Poem for Paddy O'Sullivan 123
Poem for The Governor Of Arizona 104
Poem for the Poet the Working Man and the
      Upper Mobile Yuppie 118

Poem for the Poet Waiting On Fame	*82*
Poem for The Poets Who Feast On the Flesh of the Dead	*96*
Poets unite	179
Post Office Reflection	*65*
rain-drops seek refuge	182
Random Word Poem	*160*
Remembering	*48*
Remembering My Grandmother	*133*
Returning Home From Panama	*120*
San Francisco Blues	*141*
San Francisco isn't what	78
San Francisco Streets	*61*
Saturday Night Happenings	*47*
Saturday Night Special	*46*
Seven months into	151
Seventy	*156*
Seventy-One	*157*
She sits alone	76
she sits alone in her small	55
Sitting alone at	53
Sitting at the 3300 Club	*76*
sitting here alone	114
Six AM Poem	*95*
Smell of spring in the air	162
Snow light warm dream	160
snuck into your bedroom while	112
so many hospitals with	168
Some people guard their lives	118
some things stick in your mind	170
Sometimes the Words Just Won't Come	*112*
South of Market	*50*
South of Market Blues	*66*
State of Affairs	*110*
stepped on pissed on	101
Strange this trip back in time	163
Survival Song	*92*

Tenderloin Cafeteria Poem | *117*
Tenderloin Cafeteria Poem II | *100*
Thank God for Small Favors | *63*
The coin disappears | 77
the drums beat slowly | 60
The girls of the Tenderloin | 71
the night brings no pain | 63
The old Black Hawk booked | 54
the old men of Aquatic Park | 139
The words come harder | 156
There is this certain | 96
There is this small press magazine | 146
these bars are all the same | 98
these old men beat | 97
They cross the border looking | 104
They had this bar | 120
They're having a rumble | 64
Thinking About Then and Now | *119*
This poem is for you | 59
This poem is for you | 92
Thoughts on the California Drought | *113*
Tossing turning | 154
Trump Land | *184*
tuned in the television set | 122
turn the radio off | 99

Un Titled | *109*
Under the Light of a Full Moon | *88*

Vietnam Winter Reflections | *122*
visions of the past float | 128

Walking the Mission on a Hot Sunday Afternoon | *84*
Walking the Streets Like a Cowboy Looking for a Miracle | *85*
Waste Land of Blurred Visions | *176*
Wasted Days of Wasted Nights | *98*
we live on marked time | 138
We made love in this house | 111

When I was young   68
when I worked in Modesto   119
Winter Poem   *158*
Winter Poem II   *182*
Woman on the Balcony   *73*
Worlds Last Rodeo, The   *163*
Wrong Side of Town, The   *45*

you can find them   149
You can see from   50
You can't escape it   86
You see them coming   51
You think you know me because   143

40th Birthday Poem   *80*
66   *155*

ABOUT THE AUTHOR

A.D. Winans

A.D. Winans is an award winning native San Francisco poet and writer. His poetry, articles, fiction and reviews have appeared in nearly 2000 literary magazine, journals, newspapers and anthologies including *City Lights Journal, New York Quarterly, Poetry Australia, Beatitude, Beat Scene, American Poetry Review, The San Francisco Chronicle* and *The Outlaw Bible of American Poetry*. He was a friend of Beat poets Bob Kaufman and Jack Micheline, and appears in the Kaufman documentary film, *When I Die I Will Not Stay Dead*, that premiered at the 2016 San Francisco International Film Festival. He is the author of over sixty books and chapbooks of poetry and prose and edited and published *Second Coming Magazine/Press* from 1972 through 1989. In 2002 a song poem of his was performed at Alice Tully Hall in NYC. In 2006 he was awarded a PEN National Josephine Miles award for excellence in literature. In 2009 he was presented with a PEN Oakland Lifetime Achievement Award. In 2015 he was the recipient of a Kathy Acker Award in poetry and publishing.

www.ingramcontent.com/pod-product-compliance
Lightning Source LLC
Chambersburg PA
CBHW080502110426
42742CB00017B/2975